Father's Day

A Memoir

DEDICATION

For Lucy; for everything.

I never saw a wild thing sorry for itself; a small bird will drop frozen dead from a bough without ever having felt sorry for itself.

D. H. Lawrence

Some of the best things that have happened to us would never have happened, but for some of the worst things that have happened to us.

ALL profits from this publication shall be shared between the Katie Piper Foundation (Registered charity: 1133313) and Frenchay After Burns Children's Club (Registered Charity No. 1105104)

Disclaimer

Apart from very minor changes to some names and locations the following is a true account of the events described herein.

No part of this book may be reproduced, or stored in a retrieval system, or transmitted in any form or by any means, electronic, mechanical, photocopying, recording, or otherwise, without the express written permission of the publisher.

Other Books by the Author

*The Execution,
Life and Times of Patrick O'Donnell*

Jack Has Got Your Tongue

Never be Unkind to a Waitress

My First Pipe Bomb

Mini Driver

A Boy is Not Just for Christmas

The Plank

Cover artwork; Kirsty O'Donnell
28 March 1987 to 17 June 1990.
By Kevin Sinnott: Reproduced with his kind permission.
© Kevin Sinnott.

Copyright © 2022 Gavin O'Donnell
ISBN: 9798803167969

Introduction

There was no going back into the inferno, not again; as dreadful as it was even to contemplate, I knew that the obstacle over which I had tripped had been my daughter Kirsty's lifeless body.

So started the first day of our first family holiday, the last day of our old lives; June 17th 1990; Father's Day.

I still find it difficult to speak of that night, even to my wife, and she can't easily hear it; but I found I can write about it, and she can read it, she can read what we both can't easily say, even now, 32 years after we lost our precious daughter Kirsty.

We don't want sympathy, that least of all; maybe a little understanding, maybe the realisation that we are like you and you are like us, chance and fate is all that separate us.

This memoir is my account of the worst day of our lives, and the many bad days that followed, but also of some of the best days of our lives… from the despair and pain that followed the accident, to the wonder and unbelievable joy of when our son opened his eyes after three months in a coma, and recovery started for us all.

I will take you to my childhood, to our meeting, and our lives as they are now. It's not all about the accident, but like it or not, since that day, things did change, we changed, everything changed in our world; how could it not?

Father's Day

Chapter One

Gavin
Sister, Sister - (1971)

I would like to introduce you to me, 10-year-old me. An age when I thought I carried all the troubles of the world, but in fact I carried none.

To set the scene; it's 1971 or maybe 72, and the world has an innocent face. Summers are long and warm; winters are white and cold. Portly coppers cuff kids for scrumping apples, pubs shut at eleven and supermarkets don't yet exist.

Coercive control and the environment are unknown, and priests have nice hats, which good children never touch. Few people have coloured TVs and coins are changing shape. It's a lovely, happy time of flares and platform shoes, Gary Glitter and friendly disc jockeys who do a lot for charity.

Radio Luxembourg, promises an improved signal, but it never comes. I listen to it anyway on my tiny transistor with a low battery, under the pillow.

Kids play 'down the woods' and on the railway lines, and only come home when they are hungry or it's dark. Mums make 'bangers and mash' and dads smoke pipes, in front of two-bar heaters, maybe watching Alf Garnet, and his humorous take on life; 'observational comedy'… apparently.

It is from this era that I have one of my most distinct childhood memories, though not the earliest; that is in chapter three.

I was about 10 years of age and sitting in the school's office, which served as an anteroom to Sister Agatha's lair. I wore a V neck pullover, grey knee length shorts, brown sandals and grey socks. I know this not because of great recall, but because it was the uniform for Saint Francis Catholic primary School in Milford Haven; the place where I had the misfortune to be located, for several of my formative years.

I do remember however that my socks always drooped around my ankles, the elastic having given up during my brother Edward's prior ownership of the uniform, and possibly Will's before that. I hated having to pull them up, so I used to tie string around my calf to hold them fast, but it never worked for long and the string made my legs sore.

It's not that we were poor, we were not. It's just that no one in those days threw away clothes which still had some use left in them. It was a way of life for most people in the sixties and seventies, long before it became the notion of 'socially aware' influencers on social media. What will they think of next? Baking instead of buying cakes perhaps?

My pullover too was ill fitting, and was long past its best. On its left breast was the 'Saint Francis School' logo, hand stitched badly and not quite straight. The sleeves were too long and covered most of my hands. To hide this, I developed the habit of walking around with my arms behind my back, like a miniature scholar. A hole had worn in both folds of one cuff and my thumb protruded through as if it were a tramp's mitten. It's funny how some little things come to mind and the bigger things escape one's reminiscence completely. I was acutely aware, and sort of ashamed, that my uniform was a little threadbare, but looking back I am sure no one else even noticed.

In common with many pupils at Saint Francis, I was no stranger to the headmistress's office and the compulsory wait outside, nor, to be fair, was I a very frequent visitor either. The mandatory, temporary confinement to the anteroom was presumably intended to add gravity to the ordeal, as though I needed reminding just how serious my offence had been.

It is commonly believed that teachers knew little of the psychology of children until the nineties, my experience suggests that the nuns at Saint Francis were experts in the field long before. The expectation of punishment and the guilt after it, were often as bad as the punishment itself; indeed, these aspects seemed integral to the effective and holy chastisement of 10-year-olds.

Although I was not an achiever academically, or even average, I was for the most part pretty well behaved, and my occasional scrapes with the nuns, who ran the place, tended to be on the low end of the criminal spectrum. I even served as an altar boy in the church which was located at the bottom of the school's drive.

Once every week and again on 'holy-days', which seemed to me to occur far too often, the whole school would traipse two by two down the new tarmac drive to the church; hands joined, palms together, fingers pointing heavenward, with nuns placed intermittently along the line, presumably to prevent a rush for the hills to secular and educational freedom.

Located conveniently next to the church, was the parish priest's parochial house, from whence, I was now assured by Sister Agatha, the priest had been summoned.

The teaching and administrative faculty (or 'The God Squad' as we called them) consisted almost entirely of nuns, not just any old nuns, but to me at least, what seemed to be the most awful nuns ever to have taken holy orders.

My teacher for part of that year, and all the year before had been Sister Agness, and I confess that I did not like her one bit.

I should say that this is not the impression all the pupils had of Sister Agness. As an adult some years after leaving school I spoke to several ex-pupils who remembered her, not kindly, but not with the same fear and dislike I had for her. The women in particular, who had been in her class years before, seemed to find her and the other nuns, much more agreeable than I did. I can only speak for what I experienced and felt. I accept that some did not have it as hard as I did, but also, I know for sure that others had it far worse.

Father's Day

By the time I was 10 or 11, I had been at Saint Francis for a few years - since my father relocated to the dredging works at Milford Haven docks. As a result of his occupation my siblings and I were dragged from one location to another, often far-flung places, the most recent before Milford Haven being Algeria.

Having returned from Africa three years earlier, aged about 6 or 7, I struggled with English, as I had been taught in the medium of French until then. Until age five I had also been an elective mute, I have no idea why. Consequently, all efforts were concentrated on my spoken English and little else, so by the time I was 11 I could hardly read at all. At the time I found this intensely embarrassing.

This, for reasons I never could fathom, seemed to delight Sister **Agness**. In my previous year she would regularly ask me to stand up in class to read from my stage one reading book, this to my acute shame; as the rest of the class were many stages ahead when it came to reading.

In my final year of primary school, I had not escaped her, as she regularly took our class for some subject or other. I have no idea why, maybe she just could not let go of our relationship.

Sister Agness was a stout overweight, solid, red-faced bitch. She, like all the 'penguins', wore full black habit including coif and wimple. Slung about her neck was a rosary with a large wooden cross at its end. She smelled strongly of moth balls and had the beginnings of a white beard. She might have been forty years old or eighty, as far as I could tell at the time, but looking back, she was probably in her late middle age, old enough to have nothing to look forward to and young enough to regret 'her' life 'choice' and lament what she might have had.

Her modus operandi never changed. I would struggle through the words, desperately staring at the letters as if by some miracle they would suddenly crystallise into meaningful text. Even if they did, I still would have been at a loss. She would walk slowly past, swinging her rosary, not entire rotations, just half swings like a priest with incense… and then she would turn to look over my shoulder, and read the words loudly for me to repeat. I was never swift enough or loud enough, and always the same result ensued. First the moderate abuse;

'Are you stupid booooy? Cat got your tongue booooy?'

Only for her to finish with a swing of the rosary, this one an entire loop, to land the wooden cross square into the back of my head. The sound of the impact seemed to ring hollow, confirming Sister Agness' and my father's relentless assurances that my head was in fact empty.

It was not so painful, after all I had grown up with a father who could, and occasionally did, knock me off my feet with a head shot and an open palm. It was the humiliation; I used to worry desperately how my classmates must regard me?

It would be another four years before I turned on such cruelty, though not from a nun, but for then, in this class of thirty-two children and one monster, I had no choice but to suffer the humiliation with the humility of a good Catholic boy.

My treatment at the hands of Sister Agness was all the more perplexing to me at the time because by contrast the nuns who taught my brothers and me in Algeria, only a few years earlier, were kindness incarnate. My youngest brother at the time was Roger, he and I had been taken under their wings; the only two white faces in the class. In the hot afternoons we were given the best shaded seats under the fig trees in the school's courtyard, and allowed to sleep in class when the other children were not, presumably because unlike us, they were used to the heat. I had expected the nuns at Saint Francis to be the same or at least to exhibit some kindness. They did not, at least not to some of us.

I was a child of course, and did not realise that I need not have worried about what my classmates thought, because like me, most of them had their heads down and faces front, lest they invoke the wrath of God, through his humble and devoted servant, Sister **Agness**, and her wooden cross. They each had problems of their own.

Children often do not realise others have problems and they tend to worry about all the wrong things. Henry O'Sullivan for example would wet himself regularly in class, because he was too terrified to put his hand up to ask to go to the toilet. Kids like Henry knew not to draw attention to themselves; Henry knew better than most. Sister Agness used to make him sit in his urine until break time when he was allowed to make the walk of shame to the secretary's office, to be given spare trousers. You might be surprised at the prevalence of trouser wetting in a Catholic primary school in the early seventies… or you might not, that would depend on how blind your faith is. It's good the nuns had such a large supply of pants.

Returning home to face his parents, with his wet clothes in a bag was an experience about which only Henry could testify, but of course never would. The regular bruising and absences from school spoke enough of Henry's home life. Silence, next to ignorance and obedience had for so long, and for so many, been the bedfellows of abuse, in schools, in the church and at home. Saint Francis was no different. It's hard to imagine in these enlightened times that fifty years ago such abuse was not just overt, but actually used as a deterrent for any other child who might consider pissing his pants in class.

These days, when collecting my grandson from school I often hear clueless parents complaining about arrangements for lunch, uniforms, school trips, the school bus or some other thing, and wish they could realise what fantastic, inclusive, wonderful places primary schools are these days, in comparison to what they were.

Henry was from a desperately poor Irish immigrant family. His hair was shaved up the sides and the back of his head, leaving a thick unwashed copper coloured tuft at the top. He was deeply freckled giving the impression of stained skin, and I used to think that the 'discolouration' was due to the amount of pee he had, over the years, spilled down his legs. He continually stank of stale piss, fear, aggression and desperate unhappiness. Henry was my best friend.

How much worse was his life than mine I wonder? Henry's world at the time never featured much in my contemplations, nor therefore, I suppose did my world in his, or in others'. Looking back over the years, I can see that it is likely no one knew of my embarrassment about reading, but at the time it did not seem so. To me it was everything, and I dreaded school and hated it ever since. Even now I cannot read out loud, or stand and give a presentation, though thankfully I can read, albeit slowly. Subtitles on TV are a waste on me but books are a joy. I wish I could claim dyslexia or some other explanation, but I am just a very slow and non-confident reader, who loves to read!

I think I have my father to thank for that in a way; I rarely saw him without a book in his hand. All my brothers are avid readers too, as is my son… it really is the greatest gift and I think I knew it even at the age of ten, and that partly is why my inability was so hard to bear, I could see what I was missing.

Eamon, my son, as a child would read anything from a cornflakes box to Terry Pratchett. Aged 12 he asked me for Ernest Hemingway for his birthday, I asked which one, and he looked at me quizzically;

'All of them' he replied…

I love that! Not so much his appetite for good literature, but his incredulity that anyone could consider just one book as appropriate. Alas, I digress…

Back to my friend Henry, whom I have not seen in over 50 years. His cousin had been through the same treatment in school and at home as him, and when he moved up to Milford Haven Secondary School, the students took over the bullying from the nuns. He tolerated it for almost five years but with maturing age I presume came an increasing awareness of his predicament. He was sixteen years old when he was found in Blackbridge woods, he had hanged himself.

I didn't know the boy, he was in my eldest brother's class, but even now I feel sick to my stomach that anyone could feel so sad and desperate as to do that. It really bothers me, even to this day. I have no idea why but I often think of him, or maybe more the situation that allowed it to happen. Maybe it was my first exposure to how terrible the world was and is. No note, no explanation, no investigation, just the shame when the parish priest refused to bury him in consecrated ground due to the nature of his demise.

To be fair to the priest, which is against all my natural instincts… it was until 1983 forbidden by Rome to bury a suicide victim, on consecrated ground, so the priest had no choice. I use the word 'victim' intentionally – and correctly!

Thus was our little community, too many drunken abusive fathers, silent-suffering, enabling mothers, physically abused and emotionally destroyed children, and a twisted church which fed off the misery and ignorance, with its promises of salvation for those who suffer the most. A model and a lie repeated the world over, conceived in Rome, birthed and nurtured in poor communities around the globe, and exemplified in Irish expat ghettos everywhere.

As I sat outside Sister Agatha's office such philosophies did not trouble my child's mind, the questions and indeed some of the answers would arise in the years to come. Right then I was occupied with trying to come up with a good reason as to why I had stabbed Henry O'Sullivan in the ear with a pair of compasses, and thus, hopefully, reduce the tariff of lashes with the Leather, which certainly must now be due.

'The Leather' was an implement of God's and Sister Agatha's discipline. I had never seen it myself, but was sure it resided in her desk, only to be deployed in the most serious of situations. Rumour amongst the pupils suggested that it boasted an embossed cross and the letters 'I.N.R.I'... God's tool for sure.

Looking back, I don't think anyone actually ever saw it, and it almost certainly did not exist. I know they existed in the Christian Brothers Secondary schools but even Catholic educators would not so severely hurt children under 11... right? It was more than likely a myth used to subjugate us, much like the concept of God. No one knew for sure if he existed, no one had seen him, but we all knew that if he did exist, he could hurt you... badly, so best believe in him to be on the safe side. Yes - God and the leather were very similar.

The more usual means of discipline from Sister Agatha was her double ruler, the existence of which was not in any doubt. This was two wooden rulers held together and used more often than not flat across the palms. To be fair, the noise was more frightening than the blow was painful, though she was not beyond turning them and using them sideways, sometimes across the knuckles, which hurt a good deal more. Sister Agatha was only rarely seen without her rulers, most notably on open days or a parental visit.

Other pupils at Saint Francis, including my brother Edward, claimed to have seen the Leather, and if it did exist, he surely would have been a prime candidate for its acquaintance. In contrast to me, Edward was very academic but also, he really was not a well-behaved boy. It seemed to me that he spent more time in the headmistress's office than did she.

Edward's desire and attempts to thieve anything not nailed down were always thwarted by nothing other than what seemed to be his singular determination to get caught. He was inarguably, simultaneously the most prolific little thief the school had ever seen, and yet, also the least successful. Indeed, most police forces would have been proud of what seemed to be the school's remarkable detection rate. When it came to thefts, the reality was that Edward was a spectacularly useless petty crook. He had all the enthusiasm worthy of a master criminal, but alas nothing else required for the least nefarious endeavour.

This combination served our two eldest brothers, Will and Brandon, well. When a patsy was needed for their own dubious activities, there he was. The usual method practiced was to invite Edward into some minor peripheral role, and when things went wrong, to leave him with enough involvement to get the blame - and it worked. More often than not Edward would think himself the mastermind and not the patsy, which is I suppose the whole point of having a patsy.

Eventually, in school and at home, the list of crimes attributed to Edward exceeded the ones he'd actually committed by a significant margin. In fact, by such a margin that we often wondered how our father, an intelligent man, could possibly think that Edward was responsible for the many misdemeanours committed. Surely, he must have known it was not possible for one child out of seven to be the sole architect of all the mischief.

Edward passed his 'eleven-plus' a year earlier. This was effectively the entrance exam for the Milford Haven Grammar School. He therefore had escaped to the freedom of a comparatively secular education. Whilst the grammar school was ostensibly a Church of England school the emphasis on religion was not significant, just a prayer or two in assembly and compulsory religious education classes only once a week.

Ironically, due to being a Roman Catholic, Edward was excused religious instruction classes and assemblies each morning. He immediately and enthusiastically employed the extra free time getting into more trouble, mostly visiting empty classrooms, to filch anything and everything opportunity was kind enough to leave in his path.

By the time he was fourteen he seemed constantly on the promise of a term in borstal. Borstal was a place for young reprobates, something akin to a finishing school for ruffians, but without French lessons and table manners.

Everything was tried to 'straighten him', there were numerous psychiatrist evaluations, special activity holidays, violin lessons and pretty much everything else short of electrotherapy, all to no avail. On a school trip to Venice for example he had to be rescued from a balcony, I think he maybe mistook the city for Verona.

I remember he got run over by a car outside the Grammar School when he was fourteen. To be fair, that was unlikely to have been something planned by our parents, to knock the badness out of him, though on the other hand the possibility should not be completely discounted.

I remember walking home from school one afternoon and seeing the ambulance parked outside the school, and a single shoe on the road. There was some bruising and soreness but no lasting harm. Edward got a new pair of shoes as a result, and I was a little jealous. The thought of throwing myself under a car, preferably slow moving, only for a moment crossed my mind.

Unknown to anyone at the time, and possibly to Edward himself was that he was homosexual. Looking back, I attribute much of his difficulties in his youth to that single fact. Not being gay in and of itself, but much more how people and society in general reacted to that, our community in particular. Of course, in the modern enlightened times to come, this would not be an issue to most people. This however was the early 1970s and being gay in the 1970s in an Irish Catholic family was *to be avoided* if at all possible.

Apart from being gay or maybe because of it, in that time and situation, Edward was also an exceptionally square peg who was deeply troubled and I suppose he had nowhere to turn, no one to help or advise him.

By the time he was sixteen he joined the merchant navy and that proved disastrous for him. It's a pity he did not stay at school and sit A Levels and go to university. He was certainly capable, but he needed to get away as much as our parents wanted him gone… or a little less.

It's hard to say what my parents knew when he joined the merchant navy and went off to sea. I would have been about fifteen and I did not even know what gay was, let alone that it was ungodly and to be condemned and punished when possible. In retrospect it is hard for me to see how our parents did not know.

Many years later, at the age of fifty-two, Edward was found dead in a half-way house for the homeless in London. So much life and potential lost, so many years of suffering before it was physically extinguished forever. He'd choked in his sleep on his own vomit. I suppose it is some comfort to know he did not suffer, at least not in the last minutes of his life, I can't speak for the other 50 odd years, well actually I can, but that is not what this book is about.

It's a funny thing; in the past in Ireland a parent would boast of a son who had become a priest and hide the son who *had chosen* to be homosexual (the two of course not being mutually exclusive). By 2008 it was the polar opposite. Having a gay son was a mark of one's progressive and reasonable parenting and the less said about the priest the better. I wonder, do some parents now pretend to have gay offspring, and hide the deviant spawn who became a priest?

Edward and I were exceptionally close, and the more perceptive of you might detect certain anger about how he was treated by my parents. The anger is not really about how he was treated, that was the way it was in those days, the anger is about the refusal to make proper contrition. The pretence that a couple of years of acceptance, because society has changed what is and is not OK, constitute reparation for the dreadful pain caused to my brother. Yes, I am angry, bloody angry! He deserved better. As you shall read, my wife too was the object of their blind, merciless bigotry. I don't intend to write much about it, as I say; it's not what this memoir is about, but I am bound to mention it and shall do so in due course.

As kids and into his late thirties Edward and I were very close but we saw much less of each other later, mostly due to distance I suppose. I was getting on with my little family, and as you shall read had some life issues to deal with, and he lived in the big smoke, in another world altogether. It is how life goes. I regret not seeing more of him but then… given the mischief we used to indulge when we were together, maybe it's as well we did not see as much of each other later in life.

Returning to the leather; it was a thing of legend amongst the children of Saint Francis, rumours of how children had been beaten to death with it abounded. Of course, it was unlikely that any children had been thrashed to death by Sister Agatha, though I did not, as I sat outside her office, draw much comfort from this.

As I awaited my fate, my concern as to the extent of my punishment from the headmistress was dwarfed by my concern with what I would face when my father learned of the incident.

'It was an accident', never in my experience… ever, amounted to a satisfactory explanation or excuse to anyone in power, in particular not to the nuns or my father.

On the plus side however, my father always had a hiatus for several weeks after a particularly bad episode on the whisky, and only a week before he'd seriously overdone it. As a consequence, we gained a few weeks of relative peace. There could not have been a better, or perhaps least bad time to get my father involved.

I have always thought this way. After the initial realisation of a bad predicament, I immediately look to the positives, and try to build the best scenario I can, and then work to it. After my ability to sleep pretty much on demand, it's possibly the best of my few good qualities. That is not to say I am overly or unrealistically optimistic. I have never been one to think things will get better just because I want them to. Like the man taking out a payday loan thinking he will have more money down the road, but with no reason or plan to that end.

I was a grown man before I realised that this is a remarkably useful inclination, and I have to say, it has probably saved my sanity more than once. I often attribute the words I spoke to my wife Lucy on the terrible night that we lost our daughter, to that characteristic. A sort of survival mechanism I suppose; we shall come to that.

Positive thinking really does work. My thought process sitting there age just 10 or 11, was that *things could be worse*, which was and is true, things can usually be worse, but they always can get better.

The stabbing of Henry's ear was of course a complete accident. The class were being introduced to geometry, shapes and such things, and we had been put into pairs for the task. Henry and I made up one pair, as we always did. I was used to the stink of piss and actually kind of liked it in a strange way. It was sort of comforting, familiar, but not something I could ever admit. I liked the smell of old ladies too, sort of like mint imperials, coal dust and pee. I think it was from staying with my paternal grandmother in Bridgend when I was very young. Don't tell anyone, they will think me weird.

Each pair in the class were given a different instrument and asked to examine it, and then pass it around. Henry and I had a protractor and after tracing shapes around it, seeing if we could snap it, Henry tasting it, and we both examining the heck out of it generally, we passed it to the next pair.

The next instrument was a pair of compasses. I opened and closed them and was struck by the clicking noise they made. Henry was turned away passing the protractor to Judy Coal on the next desk. Keen for Henry to hear the 'cricket like' clicking I offered the compasses to his wildly protruding, freckled ear, only for him, at that moment, to turn his head back and impale his ear on the pointed end of the implement. Henry involuntarily let out a cry and within a second his ear was spouting what seemed to be his body's entire blood supply.

Nuns, in common with all religious obsessives or tyrannical rulers, love order and hierarchy. Whilst Sister Agness ran her class like a stalag and could ruthlessly dole out moderate punishments and copious humiliation and shame, there was a limit. When it came to physical chastisement, and it nearly always did, the teachers, including Sister Agness were limited to wooden rulers across the hands and bottom, board dusters and chalk thrown and even a slap across the face. Her inventive use of the wooden cross was outside of the rules, and known about, but sort of overlooked given its ingenuity and divine implications.

Due to the letting of blood, I knew that I had just exceeded the limit for local chastisement. This was going up the ranks to the top. I realised immediately that I was in big trouble and as Henry began also to realise it, for some reason, he engineered even more blood to spill from his wound, if that were possible, by pulling and squeezing his lobe.

There is something curious about children, in that somehow the more trouble into which they can land a classmate, a friend even, the more it serves them in some way. We have all seen it; a child tripped in the sand box wailing harder and higher, until the culprit is appropriately scolded, to the satisfaction of the injured party. It is a most unpleasant characteristic, but probably a necessary one for survival from an anthropological point of view. The threat must be illuminated before comfort and safety for the injured party can be enjoyed.

Whilst Sister Agness was no doubt delighted that I was for the high jump, she must to some extent, have lamented the fact that this was a class one offence, she'd not be able to enjoy a good six of the best to my open hand with her wooden ruler.

So it was that I arrived in the headmistress's office anteroom, via two long corridors, past each of the classrooms and across the assembly hall, all the way my right ear in the firm grip of Sister Agness; me tip toeing to prevent the auditory appendage being torn from the side of my head.

Ear pulling technically was not a punishment, if it was required to motivate the child to walk swiftly in a particular direction. Thus, it escaped the punishment classification which otherwise would have made it a prohibited, or at least a reserved practice. In her other hand, the one not employed

Father's Day

pulling my ear, she held the blood-stained compass aloft as though Henry's blood might somehow compromise her purity.

Upon arriving at the office, I was unceremoniously plonked down on a chair while Sister Agness knocked on the heavy oak door to the main sanctum of the school's authority.

The doors to the headmistress's office always confused me. One door opened outwards only for there to immediately be another, which opened into the office; barely four inches between them. I supposed it was something to do with privacy because, all the children, had to attend confession in the office periodically.

I hated that, not so much the act of confession; it was after all a necessary sacrament to save the rotting souls of 10 and 11-year-old children from damnation; it was the embarrassment. I had to kneel in front of the priest, and tell him my darkest secrets, face to face. It's almost as if humiliation was somehow deliberately built into the process… but that is me being cynical I guess, who on earth would get satisfaction from the humiliation of children?

To be fair, most of the priests I encountered as a child were OK. They appeared around the school now and then, but left it pretty much to the penguins. They were frightening and imposing figures in those days, especially to children, but for the most part they seemed to lack that cruel streak so prevalent in the nuns.

There was one however who made me particularly uncomfortable, I was too young to realise what it was, but I disliked the creature. He was not our usual holy man; he'd stood in for the parish priest a few times. Years later I tried to get information about him from the diocese, but they told me that records for casual stand-in priests were not kept. They apparently were often friends of the parish priests... No such thing, and indeed no need for suitability checks in 'dem days'; everyone knew priests were the good guys... Right?

I am not even sure of his name but given he is now likely dead I shall call him Father Twomey, if I am incorrect and he is still around, he can always let me know and I shall happily correct that.

What I do say with certainty, is that it was not Father Jackson, who although a fat and well-fed priest, never offended me other than by peddling his religious nonsense to his captive audience, amongst whom I had the misfortune to number.

In fact, to be fair, I remember Jackson had congratulated me at my confirmation for taking such care to select an appropriate confirmation name. It was Saint Sebastion. I had seen a picture of him full of arrows and thought he looked cool. It's funny what one remembers, but I do remember that piece of kindness, the recognition meaning so much.

I still disliked the man as he was a priest, and I guess just as a child is almost instinctively afraid of fire and of heights and of loud noise, so I am and always have been instinctively cautious of figures of authority, particularly but not exclusively religious authority.

Children I think have an intuition about many things, the problem is that they are told almost from birth to distrust it, and instead follow the rules, the adult rules, the adult priest rules. How many poor children have suffered at the hands of persons in authority and trust because they have ignored the little voice in their heads, or the knot in their stomachs, telling them something is wrong? So it was with Father Twomey, I felt very uncomfortable around him, but he was a priest… what harm?

As it happens, I had made my confession in the headmistress's office, the previous Wednesday, just two days earlier, and it had been with Father Twomey. This was regardless of the fact that my parents made me go to confession every second Saturday anyway. All good Catholic parents of good Catholic children did the same. Saturdays were fine, the confessional was in Saint Francis church, and there were proper cubicles and barriers with all the requirements for discretion.

My Saturday confession, in church four days before my Wednesday confession in school, had also been with the same priest and although I disliked him and confession generally at least it felt more normal, more official, and whilst I always hated people saying it; as a kid, I really did feel cleaner coming out of the confessional than going in.

Before the Catholic apologists jump on that as something nice, they should first consider why a 10-year-old boy should feel unclean going in, not rejoice in his belief in his cleanliness coming out. What on earth can a normal child that age do which is wrong or sinful? Forget the extreme examples; I was a pretty normal kid.

The priest knew who you were in the church confessional, but it was much less stressful when you did not need to face him. Confession in Sister Agatha's office was a dreadful ordeal. It was bad enough with the usual chap, but this stand-in was vile. As I sat awaiting my fate in that little office, I could remember how uncomfortable the last confession with him had been, it was only two days before.

'Bless me father for I have sinned.' whilst making the sign of the cross.

'Bless you my child… and how long is it since your last confession?'

I would like to have said: 'You know how long it is you fat fucker, it was Saturday and you asked me about wanking then... just like you're going to now!'

Instead, I opted for the standard;

'Four days father… these are my sins; I stole a tanner from Mam's purse, but I put it in a fruit machine in the off licence on Steynton Road and won 10 bob; so I put the tanner back into her purse and put another one in with it. She doesn't know.'

'I see my son, it is still the sin of theft and of gambling but it is good that you returned the money, on what did you spend the rest?'

'Funny Face lollies and sweets for my friends and me… father.'

'For my friends and I' corrected the priest, erroneously, apparently unaware of the difference between the subject and the object of a verb (Sister Agness would be so proud of me!).

Of course, at the time I had no idea of the rule but I did know to duck if I used 'I' instead of 'me' or vice versa in front of my father. So, I always got it right, even from a very young age. I learned to hold cutlery correctly and to stand if a woman entered the room in the same way. As I got older, my manners and grammar improved inversely proportional to having sore ears. I'm not complaining not by any means, how many of my compatriots know to serve caviar with a bone spoon, not silver, to pass port to the left, and when vomiting from too much beer to do it quietly and blame the dog?

'Gluttony too is a sin my son. Is that all?' continued the bulbous loose-double-jowled pig.

'Yes father.'

'Are you sure my son?'

'Yes father.'

'Have you been tempted to play with yourself at all my son?'

'Play with myself father?' Of course, I knew perfectly well what the priest meant. I remember looking up into the sweaty face and how I sensed the danger and decided not to play that game: 'Yes father but just once and I said a Hail Mary and an Act of Contrition after.'

'And are you sorry for your sins?'

'I am father; truly sorry.'

'The body is the vessel of Christ my son and you must not abuse it, to abuse your body is to abuse

Christ'. He paused. 'For your penance say a decade of the rosary and make an Act of Contrition.'

The priest, as usual muttered some words in Latin which apparently granted me forgiveness, he made a sweeping gesture of the sign of the cross and dismissed me. I dared not even look back at him as I left the double doored room. I instinctively disliked the man already, but there was something very creepy about the experience that day.

I was roused from my remembrance of my previous confession when the door to the office swung open. Sister Agness had already reminded me that my soul was in peril and now, accompanied by Sister Agatha they reinforced the message with a tirade of abuse and threats ostensibly for my benefit, and on behalf of the almighty, but actually for their own gratification.

Sister Agatha was a tall woman, at least to me, and in comparison, to the squat and solid Sister Agness. She had a permanently red face which looked as if she'd scrubbed her skin with a scouring pad, or was about to explode. She was much calmer than the other penguins however, but equally as unkind. They almost all had that defect, but there was at least some logic to her cruelty. For example, when my eldest brother attended the school, she would beat him across the knuckles with the edge of her double-barrelled rulers. He was bright and excelled in class, but he was left-handed. She did this every time she caught him writing with his left hand. To this day his writing, now only done with his right hand, is illegible. That said, my own is also illegible and I never got struck on the hand while writing, just the head.

Of course, in the real world this was cruel and destructive, but to her it was not, she sincerely believed that to use one's left hand to write was sinister; the left-hand being Satan's tool. This was never actual official church doctrine or had not been for a few hundred years. The church simply provided enough evidence and comment so as to leave no other reasonable inference for the devout to *draw*.

Sister Agatha did not like me, but her dislike was manifest more in distain than any overt cruelty. She disliked my whole family as it happened. Some months after my siblings and I had been accepted at the school, another family had applied to join. By coincidence this was the O'Sullivan family, my friend Henry's kin. Sister Agatha met the parents and decided there was no room at the school, yet, within a couple of weeks another family, the Barnetts arrived and all of them had been given places.

The Barnett family were well to do, the father was a 'professional' of some kind, and they had Imperial Leather soap in a downstairs toilet. One of my friends was invited to a birthday party at their house, and he saw it in a porcelain soap dish next to the sink. I can't remember ever being asked to a birthday party, let alone a posh one.

The Barnetts were the sort of family that Sister Agatha wanted in her school, the O'Sullivans were not. My mother, in common with all the mothers, knew of this decision, and she demanded a meeting.

At the meeting she called Sister Agatha, a hypocrite to her face. The O'Sullivan family were offered places within a few days.

Bully nuns are no different to any other bullies. If they are stood up to, they generally cower, and so it was with Sister Agatha, who was used to pushing around the local peasantry, so when she came up against someone well-travelled, reasonably educated and strong (in her own way) she showed her true colours pretty swiftly.

So here was Sister Agatha with a clear justification to open the drawer in her office and bring out the Leather.

'Gavin' she said; 'Father Twomey is on his way up to speak with you and he will help us determine what punishment you are due.'

'But Sister.' I tried.

'Silence Boy!' interrupted Sister Agness.

'But it was only an accident.' I cautiously insisted.

'Another word out of you boy and it'll be double the penance you have to pay!'

So, it was decided, I was for a thrashing come what may, from the school and more certainly from my father. I say 'thrashing' but of course it was more likely a caning, and let's not forget, not really a punishment, it was 'penance', and thus entirely for the benefit of the child, and not the satisfaction of the red-faced holy inquisitor. I knew there was no help to be had from the priest; he would only make things worse.

With that the door swung open and an out of breath Father Twomey entered. The stench of alcohol filled the room instantly. The two nuns exchanged glances and it was obvious they knew he was half, to two thirds drunk. I sat quietly trying to appear as small as possible. I did not know at the time, but this is a survival tactic of many wild animals when cornered.

Sister Agatha explained the ear stabbing situation to Father Twomey, ably assisted with timely and vigorous interjections from Sister Agness. The Priest nodded and wobbled slightly as he listened.

He was in full black cassock which was intermittently stained; no doubt from food which had escaped his jowls and fallen into his lap. It buttoned up the front from his ankles to his fat neck.

He was a tall man, and massively overweight. His face was bulbous with a double chin; his nose was like a massive over ripe strawberry, with skin peeling from it. His cheeks were bloated with what appeared to be hundreds of tiny blue veins just under the skin. His lips were continually wet and greasy and looked as though he might have finished off a suckling pig and a bottle of port without the use of a napkin. He was in every way a Catholic Priest, a caricature of himself.

Presumably he had just come from some baptism or extreme unction. Coming in, or going out of this life as a good Catholic requires a little Latin and a fat bastard to see all is compliant with God's laws. It can't have been a marriage because even my crime would not cleave him from free food and wine. It was probably the sort of event where upon concluding his most holy activity, a handful of notes would have been thrust upon him by some thankful and devout parishioner, only no doubt, for the holy man to refuse, Caesar-like, and unconvincingly, just enough times to keep the money, and appear worthy of the robes he so amply inhabited.

It's a funny thing, but I am certain that just like mediums and psychics who peddle their filth to the desperate and the stupid, in the absolute and certain knowledge that it is all nonsense, so priests do exactly the same thing. No way can anyone who has actually studied religion, believe in it, so all priests, in my respectful opinion, are deluded or liars, or both.

Upon conclusion of the report Sister Agatha dismissed Sister Agness, instructing her to attend to her class. Sister Agness backed out of the room, half bowing to the priest in a fashion worthy of Uriah Heap, though she resisted rubbing her chubby hands together.

It was thankfully by my left ear that Sister Agatha dragged me through the doors and into her office. I felt sure had she grabbed my already stretched right ear, it may well have detached, making a compass injury look, by comparison, a rather minor event.

She requested that the priest make his inquisition into the matter and confirmed she would be waiting in the anteroom, ready to administer what punishment was deemed necessary by the sagacity of the inebriated fat bastard. Though, to the best of my recollection, she possibly did not articulate it quite so.

The headmistress's room measured maybe twelve foot by twelve foot. Almost in the centre of the room was her throne, a large oak pedestal desk with green leather inlay. Upon it lay books and papers in tidy piles. A Montblanc ink pen lay next to an ink well. It occurred to me that had it been Edward in the room with the priest, Sister Agatha may well not have left such a fine pen unguarded. In fact, since my brother moved from Saint Francis the school was probably on a 'stand down' situation on the security front.

I knew what a Montblanc was because my father had been given one as a gift by a company named Atlas Simpco, which he had recommended for a contract with his employer. It was, albeit for a very short time, his most prized possession; he was very proud of it. The pen had gone missing a few weeks after it was given to him and thereafter for years, whenever drunk, which was often, he would periodically and arbitrarily punish any of us close to hand for having stolen it. Edward, naturally enough, always got the worst of it, probably with good reason but possibly not. I know I did not pinch it for sure but I got plenty of punishments for it. The theft that just keeps giving, I guess. There too on the desk sat the offending weapon; the pair of compasses, open and obviously to constitute exhibit one.

A large wooden chair with a brown leather seat was positioned against the party wall facing the desk and a few feet from it. It was obviously reserved for the exclusive use of someone very important. Only one other chair occupied the room and that was pushed under Sister Agatha's desk.

Above the desk and hanging from the wall, was a large wooden cross, next to it was a framed picture of the Sacred Heart, complete with the little red electric candle light supported on an arm at the bottom, and attached to the frame.

The flame seemed to flicker and I could not work out if it was meant to do that, or had been wired-in badly. I held briefly to a vague hope it was the latter and somehow the school might burn down as a result. OK, I admit that occasionally I am given to wild optimism. To be fair my nan had the same picture in her living room and the light on that flickered too, before it shorted and went out forever. No, regrettably not a religious message, just the nature of filaments.

As the second of the doors shut loudly behind the headmistress Father Twomey plonked himself onto the leather seat and farted loudly; he beckoned me to kneel in front of him. This was the usual position for confession in the office, but I had not really been certain I would have to make yet another one.

Even in consideration of my newfound discovery of masturbation, I was unlikely to have 'abused the temple of Christ' since the last confessional encounter, two days previous. Regardless, I supposed that acquiescence would be the route to least punishment, so I took the position without questioning.

I waited to be told what to do next. The smell of stale alcohol and rancid fart was almost overpowering yet, the dreadful, foul, sewer stench of the priest's breath took the unpleasantness to another level. I was sure I was going to puke... *For Christ's sake*, I thought, *I can't puke on a priest, not after stabbing Henry in the ear.*

It was obvious that confession was required so I proceeded in an effort to get it done with;

'Bless me father for I have sinned.' I breathed in through my mouth. I could taste the awful odour.

'And have you been touching yourself my son?' came the reply.

I was taken aback, I knew things were not right but this; so fast, no preliminaries no introduction, just straight to it. That instinct, that thing that says *run, move, get away*, kicked in immediately, I felt it in my gut, and heard it in my head. The atmosphere in the room changed in a moment; yet… this was a priest. So, I did as I was taught, I suppressed my urge to run, or to question. I was silent, but that thing in my belly, that frightening thing, of which I was not frightened, was unmistakably making its way up from my guts to my chest.

The priest asked again, slurring;

'Have you been abusing that vessel of Christ my boy?'

I noticed that his hand was beneath his tunic. It was moving. I caught a glimpse of it and looked down. My guts were on fire; I had no idea what to do or where to look. Strangely I was not afraid though, not of the priest, maybe I was afraid of the situation but not of him, I just did not know what to do next.

The priest took my right hand and placed it into his lap, forcing me to touch him; the robe parted between the buttons. I was horrified; instinctively my left hand went to the desk, in order to raise myself up from the kneeling and vulnerable position, by accident it landed on the compasses. With a single sweeping movement, half standing and half kneeling I withdrew my right hand, leaving the priest's appendage exposed, and drove the point of the implement hard into his thigh. I had aimed for his worm, but I think in the last moment I lost my nerve, and impaled the inch long point deep into the top of his thigh instead.

He screamed with pain and shock. He leapt to his feet; the compasses still embedded firmly in his leg. Thankfully his penis had made a hasty retreat to cover. I stood and backed up against the desk, my hand falling on the beautiful black pen, which, for some reason I cannot even now explain, I slipped into the pocket of my shorts. *In the midst of chaos comes opportunity*. I did not think that at the time but wish I had... I was after all just an illiterate Catholic child.

The door burst open - Sister Agatha looked at the dancing priest and then at me. She was utterly confused for a moment, until, she saw the measuring implement still firmly embedded in the now slightly more 'holy' man.

'You little fecking heathen, you'll burn in hell for this you little fecker!' shouted the priest in what was a previously well concealed Dublin accent… as he was persuaded back into his special seat, by Sister Agatha.

Apparently, regardless of context, if a priest or in fact anyone from Ireland says 'feck' it never means 'fuck', I think Twomey definitely meant 'fuck'!

The pig priest pulled a flask from his pocket and greedily drank down whatever was inside. Some spilled down over his fat cheek. I suspect that it probably was not holy water.

The screaming was heard by Mr Evans, who had just started choir practice in the adjacent hall. He was the only non-priest, non-nun in the school, and a teacher whom all the pupils, including me, adored. He burst in and witnessed the scene. I looked up at Mr Evans, and he seemed to be about to burst into laughter.

'Get that little prick out of my sight!' screamed the priest.

I was dragged from the scene, fortunately not by either ear, just as the extraction occurred, and was accompanied by screams which could be heard throughout the entire school and beyond. It was probably just a whimper but I prefer to remember it thusly.

I was placed back in the classroom where Mr Evans exchanged a few words with Sister Agness, who looked horrified, and they then both left, Sister Agness turning at the door only to say:

'Jenny O'Boyle, you're in charge,'

A comment which caused Judy Coal to frown at her classmate. Judy Coal was the best reader in the class, and usually she was put in charge when Sister left the room.

When Sister Agness returned 10 minutes later, the class resumed as normal, other than the fact that she avoided any eye contact with me, which was unusual, because staring down children was something of a hobby of hers.

It was about fifteen minutes before home time when I was summoned back to the headmistress's office. As I entered the anteroom Mr Evans was leaving. He winked at me. Though Mr Evans had always been kind I had expected a whack across the head as a minimum, not a wink.

I went into the room and turned to close the doors.

'Leave it open.' she said.

There was nothing in her voice that I could use to determine what fate was ahead.

Expulsion as a minimum I figured, *probably excommunication* from the one and only holy and apostolic church too. In fact, I was surprised not to see the bishop and some police in the office, even my father or the Pope himself.

Sister Agatha stood up; she picked up the compasses from the desk and handed them to me.

'See that Sister Agness gets this back before you go home.'

'Yes Sister' I replied. I looked at her and was flabbergasted to see her eyes deeply reddened; I had

Father's Day

seen my mother enough times to know when tears were being hidden.

'Dismissed,' she said and I turned to leave.

'You' - she paused, seemingly unable to speak further.

I stopped without turning around to face her. I didn't like the nuns at the best of times, but I liked less things I did not understand, and I did not understand gentleness from them or vulnerability in them. It was a situation I could not fathom, and I just wanted to be out of there. She composed herself behind me and did not ask me to turn.

'You will not speak of what happened today – ever.'

I was unsure if it was a question or an instruction, and didn't care.

I turned to look at her;

'No Sister, never.' and I could have sworn she smiled - a tiny uplift at the corner of her mouth.

I turned again without being invited or instructed to do so, and walked back to class, one hand holding the compasses, the other in my pocket wrapped around my new Montblanc Meisterstück 149 ink pen.

As I entered the class Sister Agness called me to the front. The other children although keen to know what punishment I had received from the headmistress for spiking Henry, were more concerned with the Friday afternoon bell. As I handed the compasses to her, she said;

'Thank you,' without looking at me, and that was that.

It would be many years before I realised what had probably happened and what had maybe been happening. In 1972 the idea that a priest might be a base creature, taking advantage of children who could turn no place, because they would never be believed, was of course unheard of, now we all know it was pretty much in the job description.

My curiosity about it all in that moment, and at that time, was outweighed by my relief knowing that I was going to live another day. I knew my parents would only be involved if I involved them, and there was no way on earth I was going to do that. Not only had I stabbed Henry in the ear accidentally, but I had deliberately stabbed a priest in the leg, and I was off scot-free. A very, very good start to the weekend for me, all things considered.

Father Twomey was never seen in the parish again, at least not by me; not in school, in mass or confession. Later I learned that it was church policy to move such beasts to pastures new, rather than punish or defrock them. No one spoke again about the incident, and I decided it probably was best not to bring it up myself, even with my brothers, with whom I shared most secrets.

Although it was only another month or so until I was finished in Saint Francis, I was never again asked to read in class.

The entire school was tasked with searching for the missing pen. We spent a whole day searching from the playing fields to the bottom of every desk and drawer in the school; all to no avail. The standard:

Father's Day

'Return it discreetly and there will be no punishment' promise was employed, in person, at assembly, by Sister Agatha, who held my gaze uncomfortably long as she made the commitment; but still, no pen ever turned up. I remember thinking that I was probably off to hell for stealing from a nun, maybe I am. I did confess the crime in confession about a week later and Father Jackson told me I'd only be forgiven if I gave it back; I never did though. I knew perfectly well that for certain Sister Agatha knew I had it, but could not say so or how she knew; so much for the sanctity of confession.

I held onto the Montblanc and still have it. I use it very rarely and for special occasions. Most recently, almost fifty years later in 2016, I used it to sign my application for the role of Magistrate in South Wales, and thoroughly enjoyed the irony, regretting only that I could not share it.

Of course, I failed the eleven-plus exams and was assigned to a class for low achievers in Milford Haven Secondary School, where I started in the following autumn. It was as expected given my standard of reading. My parents had as little expectation of me as I had of myself, I was unsure as to which expectation informed which, but I can now as an adult, hazard an 'educated' guess.

During the intervening summer holidays, I underwent extra reading lessons for slow readers. Two hours a day for the whole six-week break while my friends got to make dens and bonfires down the woods. It did not ruin the entire break but did part of it.

Unbeknown to me at the time, I benefitted from the fact that, as a parting gift, Sister Agatha had me classed as Educationally Subnormal, or 'ESN' as it was called. No euphemisms in those days for a slow reader, or someone not up to speed. I was not 'challenged' or on any spectrum, I was officially 'as thick as two short planks', as my father so often reminded me.

Far from being a spiteful act by the chief penguin it had apparently been a significant act of consideration, perhaps even, in some ways, an act of contrition. Without being so classed I would not have got the extra help and I may well have never learned to read properly, and been consigned to the dunces' class for the rest of my education.

As it happens, and as a result of me mastering reading, I was in the lower form in secondary school for just a day, before being moved up to the 'B' form. Thus, my journey in secondary education from B to A form in Milford Haven Secondary, and onto Whitland Grammar School, and eventually to my first degree in Construction Management and later my Batchelor of Laws began. Heck one day not only would I be able to read, but maybe also to write. You decide.

The upshot of all this, as you can deduce, was that thanks to the considerable efforts of my tutor, I read my first 'proper' book in its entirety by mid-August of that year. It was *Great Expectations*; it took a while but I got there and I actually enjoyed it. I've read it many, many times since. It's such a great book, perfect for a child. There are so many great books, mostly written before the invention of literary agents it has to be said.

Looking back, I have no doubt that the nuns were capable of kindness, all humans are, and as I have said, I am sure that some pupils' memories of their time at Saint Francis School will be better than mine. My memories in the playground, where I learned how to frown are good, as they are of school dinners. I used to love the days we had rice pudding because Edward never ate his, so I got it, and on lemon meringue days he got my pudding because I disliked it and he loved it. What was I thinking?

I also loved the end of term nativity play. With the proximity of the end of term behind us and of Christmas ahead it was an exciting time. One year Henry and I got to play sheep and, in another year, we were both rats in the *Pied Piper of Hamelin*. Funnily enough neither of us ever got to play Jesus or the Angel Gabriel; that tended to be the likes of Tim Barnett and others who no doubt have better memories of the school and the nuns than I have.

So, whilst there were lots of good things, they do not unfortunately define my time there. Sister Agness, making me read in front of the class, comes to mind before double helpings of rice pudding. On the whole I am glad I attended St Francis and it maybe did me more good than harm. I know for example to keep my children away from priests, and I have a nice pen to show for my time there, but it was not a pleasant experience at the time.

As soon as I got the basics of reading it became my favourite pastime. There is definitely something in the notion that the love of reading is set by example. As I have said, my dad was an avid reader as were most of my brothers, as is my son.

Most of my life I have enjoyed reading and I think this is especially so because I clearly remember not being able to read, and the feeling not just of embarrassment, but of missing out on what others took for granted. Later in life, as you shall read, I suffered some mental health trauma and one of the worst things about it was that for long periods I simply could not read. Not an inability to actually read, but a lack of concentration. It comes and goes but I am glad to say that at the moment I am half way through the autobiography of Ulysses Grant… It's not very well written, for reasons you'll understand if you read it, but it's exceptionally interesting. Reading is like education, a great leveller of man.

My favourite place to read that summer had been down at the old cast iron sewer pipe, which served as a footbridge for the kids between the Bunker's Hill Estate and Blackbridge Woods. The forty-eight-inch pipe had leaked effluent for decades and the ground for half an acre around it had turned into a deep, stinking slurry pond. The slurry was approximately level with the centre of the pipe, thus leaving a semi-circular 'run' or 'plank' across the hazard. We kids would throw stones, and breeze blocks swiped from the nearby building sites into the

Father's Day

boggy mass from the top of the pipe, and delight as the objects slowly disappeared.

Whilst it was an odorous and unpleasant place, it was quiet, and I liked it there. I was used to strange smells. The banks each side were covered in ferns, and I could sit peacefully amongst them.

I'd been so proud of finishing my first proper book that I used to carry it around with me, even when playing down the woods. By the end of the summer, it was more than a little battered, having been read and re read a dozen times. It never occurred to me to return it to the public library, from where it was borrowed by my mother.

A few days before the end of the holidays I was sitting amongst the ferns reading 'my' book when Judy Coal appeared from the woods and began to taunt me about my reading. I think she fancied me, or hated me; with kids it is hard to tell. Come to think of it, it doesn't get easier as you get older.

I walked out onto the old pipe and met her halfway; she grabbed at the tattered old book and pushed at me. As a result of her nasty disposition and in accordance with Newton's third law the book ripped in two, one half in my hand and the other in hers, as the best reader in the class fell backwards into the bog.

I, momentarily taken aback by the situation, looked down at her. My expectation, and clearly hers, was that she was going to sink like a pretty breeze block, but she did not, not completely that is. Her pelvis and her feet went down rapidly when she tried to get up, but not too deeply. Her elbows too sank but her head and shoulders were clear and elevated. She looked up at me, terrified, afraid to move.

With an acceptable delay to gather my thoughts, I took off my jumper and threw the petrified bully one sleeve. In no time I had hoisted her onto the pipe and to safety. She was covered from head to toe in partially decomposed shit, which still stank of non-decomposed shit. She had lost a shoe but incredibly had managed to hold onto her half of the book.

I escorted the weeping shit-pile to our house, where my mother washed her and phoned her mother before putting her clothes into our new automatic washing machine. My father often boasted that we were the last in the estate to have a colour TV but the first to have an automatic washing machine, I am still not sure which fact was worthy of a boast.

Pretty much certain of a confinement to bed, or to the back garden by way of punishment, I made my way to the woods to make the best of it, before sentence was handed down by my father. Oddly however it never came to that. For some reason Judy did not land me 'in the shit' as I had her; though to be fair it was a joint enterprise. It seems she told her mother that the fall had been an accident, which it actually was, and that I had happened along to help. Perhaps she had a father like mine, and she realised that she carried some of the blame. Who knows?

Her mother, by way of thanks to me for helping her daughter, bought us tickets to the Saturday matinee; the film was Tarzan, which by coincidence had a scene of a person being rescued from quick sand. During the show I wanted to kiss Judy but could not summon up the courage; she smelt of shampoo and no longer of shit. It was the last time I saw her, other than in mass in Narberth now and then. She had gone to the grammar school and I went to the secondary modern. She was after all the best reader in the class, so out of mine.

Chapter Two

Ordinary Lives
(1985 - 1990)

Things had not been plain sailing for Lucy and me after we were married in Stroud Registry Office in 1985. She, on the big day, in a blue home-made dress large enough to cover her growing bump and me in a plain grey suit. The guests were few. There was my brother Will, his wife Karen and a couple of friends along with Lucy's parents and one of her sisters, or maybe two, I can't recall.

The point of this story by the way is not to make any one feel bad, or to redress what injustice might have been done, one way or the other, but some things need to be said, to lend context.

It is with this in mind that I should mention now, and maybe again later, that my parents, devout Irish Catholics, had refused to attend the wedding. Indeed, they had completely disowned me for consorting with a divorcee, and worse, (I think) a Protestant woman… and whom my mother delicately referred to as 'soiled goods', and similarly clichéd and pejorative terms available to Catholics void of kindness, understanding and humanity.

Actually, I am not sure which was worse; 'Protestant' or 'divorced', but combined they made for my parents, and some of my family, a very toxic mix. I might add at this juncture, that next year Lucy and I celebrate our 40th wedding anniversary.

I do not suggest that longevity in a marriage is any mark of it being happy or successful, and point, ironically, to the fact that many wives stay put for extended periods of abuse, cohesive control and mistreatment, only to boast success in longevity.

When I say things were not 'plain sailing' for us I should clarify; they were good between us, always things were good in terms of the relationship. In fact, pretty much since the day we met, we have been extremely happy with each other, better than that, we like each other, which, believe it or not, is way more important than loving each other. I love several people whom I dislike.

The ink on her divorce papers hardly dry, with no engagement or wedding rings and no guest list or flowers or honeymoon, we perhaps lacked all the 'essentials' for a successful union.

As I say, we didn't have a honeymoon and it was on our 21st anniversary, while living abroad, that I finally got round to giving Lucy an engagement ring. She declared she'd have preferred the money not be 'wasted' and suggested she'd have liked much more a winter's supply of logs for the wood burners. God's honest truth that is what she said, and she meant it, and that is partly why I love her so much... and like her of course.

For the nuptials I had the day off work, after only starting my job at Berkeley Nuclear power plant a few days before. Apart from the lack of money we were optimistic and looking forward to our lives together, and very, very happy. Perhaps of all the blessings we had, that thing which would enable us to survive what was to come, was an appreciation of just how lucky we were.

That was five years before our exciting trip to France, where you, dear reader, shortly will find us, and which I shall recount to you as best I can when the time comes.

The bump in Lucy's tummy turned into our beautiful son Eamon, and he was joined a little later, in 1987 by his sister Kirsty, a blonde explosion of energy and love, the apple of my eye.

Eamon by spring of 1990 was approaching his fifth birthday and Kirsty was eighteen months younger. He adored his little sister from the moment he set eyes on her. She'd arrived in the March of 1987, and although five weeks premature she was perfect. Lucy and I used to joke that with a boy and a girl we had a 'millionaire's family' in every aspect, but for the minor detail of a million in currency.

As Kirsty grew, Eamon was ultra-protective of her and she adoring of him, looking to him for her cues in everything from singing happy birthday to me to behaving… or not… when it was their bed time.

By the time Kirsty came along things were looking promising for us as a family, and continued to improve over the few years that followed. The children were healthy and thriving, I was very happy in a new job at the hydroelectric plant in Tanygrisiau, North Wales, and had even managed to get promoted. I was on good money, and actually liked almost all of my colleagues, who seemed a very different breed to the nuclear automatons, with whom I had previously worked in Berkeley and Trawsfynydd nuclear power stations. The Simpsons, years later really did have that so right.

One setback was Lucy having a late miscarriage in 1989. It was upsetting of course, particularly for her and she'd spent most of a week in hospital, but we had two wonderful healthy children so we tried to count our blessings.

As I mentioned, my parents, did not like Lucy from the day they met her, or more accurately 'from the day they did not meet her'. Neither had allowed the fact that they had never met her to impede them forming extremely unpleasant opinions and freely expressing these to, amongst others… me. I had over the years since we married tried several times to build bridges with my parents but with limited success; almost no success really.

Although Lucy was utterly indifferent to my parent's opinion, or indeed anyone's opinion of her, she did make efforts for my sake. She had her first marriage annulled, (which is no small thing) and she converted to Catholicism. We even arranged to have the marriage convalidated in the Catholic Church, in spite of neither of us having much interest in religion, and in fact an increasing aversion to it. Short of having Lucy beatified there was little else we could have done, and I doubt that would have been enough anyway.

Unlike Lucy, I tended at the time to over-care what people thought, and for several years was upset by my parents' bigotry, but eventually I resolved to put it out of my mind. By the time I had two children I gave it as little thought as I could manage. They lived in Ireland, and we lived in the UK, so that made things less complicated.

I do not hold anything against my parents for the appalling way they treated 'soiled goods' and me... I was angry and hurt for a long time but I am past that. That is all there is to it, I really just do not care.

By the time Eamon was four years old and Kirsty was two and a half, my parents had only seen them once. It really was extraordinary. Anyone who met Lucy and spent more than five minutes in her company could not help but see what an extraordinarily good wife and mother she was, and is. There would as far as I was concerned be no more attempts at reconciliation. Events shortly to unfold took that decision out of my hands and changed it, but only temporarily.

We stayed close to my brother Will and his wife Karen who lived in Gloucestershire. They had always been particularly good to me and when I met Lucy, they accepted her without question. I mention this not because it was some extraordinary kindness, it is what one would expect, but it contrasted so much with how my parents, and others had behaved. If you detect sarcasm you are mistaken. I can't think of another way to say it. Lucy being treated as my girlfriend, and nothing more or less, was a big deal for us both.

Father's Day

Lucy's parents, who were very religious but Baptist, (may God forgive them) seemed at first ambivalent to me, cautious perhaps, and later warmed, and eventually loved us equally and were very supportive over the early years, when we were always penniless. Her father and I used to play snooker regularly in the social hall affiliated to his work. I am not sure which of us was the worst player, me I suspect.

Her father also often dropped a twenty-pound note into my hand when visiting, which was most weeks. Even when we lived in North Wales, they made the arduous round trip at least a couple of times a month to see us and the children. They were never hostile to me, though he did once tell me how disappointed he was that his daughter married a Catholic; it was in jest, I think. He also gave me a book about bad popes... I never read it; I knew enough about bad clergy already from personal experience.

Will and I often visited each other and our children got along very well with their cousins, Marie, Kate and Jake, and later William when he was born. I saw my brother Edward, a few times every year but as he lived in London it was not as regular as either of us would have liked. I had 5 brothers and a sister and I was closest to Edward due in part to our ages, but we grew apart as adults. He was ostracised from the family long before me. Being gay in an Irish Catholic family, in the mid-seventies, was not the easiest thing, I mentioned this in the previous chapter.

My only encounter in the late eighties with my youngest brother Mike, by then a young man living in London, was consequent to a late-night telephone call which required me to travel to the city to guarantee £1000 bail for him due to charges of GBH against his then girlfriend. As it turned out the long gash in Mike's face, which remains scarred to this day, was with compliments from her; courtesy of a bread knife and too much vodka. The case was eventually dropped. He since married a lovely woman, a police woman, and they have a son, and they are very happy, they live in Suffolk.

I did not mind so much standing bail for Mike, and I always had a particular soft spot for him, as he had endured living with our father during the worst times in Ireland. When we met up in the late eighties, Mike regaled me with stories of some of his own exploits over the previous few years and they included some pretty worrying antics, so I kept my distance after that, for quite a few years. I have never been sure if the exploits he boasted were real or just made up; perhaps they were exaggerated. I confess I was no angel as a teenager in Ireland so I am not judging him.

After Kirsty came along, we bought our first house, it was in Trawsfynydd in 1988 and for the next year or so we spent every spare minute and spare penny working on it, making it child safe and comfortable. We saved what we could and having had a frugal Christmas in 1989, with no family visits or bail bonds to make, by June 1990 we could afford our first family holiday. We were actually going abroad. It was very exciting for us all.

Will found a company which provided luxury camping holidays in the south of France near to Bordeaux and together we booked a week in mid-June. The campsite looked great in the brochure, with luxury tents placed in a small part of a forest which was directly on the beach front.

Eamon and Kirsty were allowed to cut out pictures from the brochure and stick them to their bed headboards weeks before we were due to travel. No internet those days. Every morning Eamon would ask;

'Are we going on holiday today?' immediately before asking 'Is today a school day?' and Kirsty would repeat the questions, looking to him for approval.

Neither Lucy nor I had been brought up on holidays. For us both, whilst growing up in Wales, day trips to the many beaches within a short drive had been our holidays, with an occasional longer trip to Tenby or Porthcawl perhaps. It was no different for my friends and I knew of no one who actually flew on an airplane for holidays.

We set off on our adventure from Trawsfynydd on a Friday morning, little knowing that we had spent our last night in the house upon which we had worked so hard, making it into a home. The blue Vauxhall with roof-box was loaded to the gunwales, both children were strapped into their seats and exploding with excitement; their little pack ups and drinks neatly stacked on the seat between them, ready for the long journey.

Eamon had a concept of what was happening and Kirsty, as always, looking to her big brother, for her cues to be over excited, was sure she did too.

The Cavalier was our fifth car, the first had been a nice Ford Fiesta which Lucy bought with her meagre divorce settlement, and had sold later to pay off my student loan in Ireland. The next car and a replacement for the Fiesta, was a very old and battered green Ford Capri Mark II. It was a wreck, the heaters didn't work at all, and there was a hole in the bulkhead. In the winter while I worked at TI Creda in Bristol, I used to wrap newspaper around my feet to stop them from freezing. For a while it fired on just three cylinders but got us around - just. Lucy was once crossing the Severn Bridge and it lost its single remaining windscreen wiper so Will drove me out to her rescue. The following week he and I stripped the top of the engine and replaced the overhead cam, which was hammering like a jack-booted rabbit in a tin box, due to lack of oil. It was a big fault on the Capri; the oil bar lubricating the overhead cam was prone to getting blocked.

I knew almost nothing about cars when we had the Capri, so I learned fast because we could not afford garage bills. Within three years I had, thanks to the help of Haynes car manuals and my greatly treasured ability to read, pretty much rebuilt the Datsun Cherry we had after the Capri and the Renault Five we had before the Cavalier,

Father's Day

The skills I picked up out of necessity in those early days proved useful later in life when, for fun, I rebuilt several old cars including a 1967 Jaguar Mark II and two 1968 Ford Capri Mark Is, my very favourite car, mainly because I can't afford a 68 Mustang.... And most have the steering wheel on the wrong side!

Chapter Three

Mohammed Ben Clecker
(1968)

Just before we go forward in time to June 1990, and to the terrible events we must inevitably explore, I would like to step back further again into my childhood; way back into my earliest memories. In this chapter I want to give you a sense of how it was growing up in my family, in my world. It's just a snapshot… it was unusual, often challenging, but believe it or not, it was in many ways the best childhood.

My family and I moved to the Bunker's Hill housing estate on the outskirts of Milford Haven in 1969 after returning from Algeria where we had spent the previous two years. I was almost eight years of age on my return from Africa and I was struggling to fit back into school in the UK. I've always hated school and I think the reason originates from that experience. As mentioned, I couldn't read and every day was an ordeal.

I'd been educated entirely in the medium of French at the Catholic primary school in Arzew. Though my speech was improving rapidly my reading skills had not been showing any signs of improvement.

I was the middle child of seven by then. The eldest brother Brandon was four years older and the leader of our little pack, the trail blazer in many ways. He'd been the first to go to primary school

Father's Day

and the first to go to secondary school, where on his first day he learned that primary school shorts to the knee were not accepted attire. He'd been the first to make his holy communion, confirmation and the first to do most things. He was also the only sibling, apart from our sister, who had the luxury of never having to wear hand-me-down clothes.

Will was the second eldest, just 11 months younger than Brandon, then Edward, who was about a year and a half older than me. Roger followed a year after me and Leonora, the only girl, was born when I was four. Mike, the last addition only came along because our parents figured they were, on the balance of probabilities, due another girl. They were wrong of course and Mike was the sixth boy and the last addition to the family.

When my youngest brother Mike was born, we were still living in North Africa and our mother had travelled back to the UK for six weeks or so to give birth there. She returned to Algeria and to seven children under the age of ten. Though thankfully, she did have a housekeeper named Hira.

In Algeria we lived in an old French colonial house. It was vast with its own courtyard and many outbuildings where my brothers and I would play. I have mixed but very limited memories of my time in Africa. I recall the Lemon trees and Lime trees lining two sides of the courtyard, the outbuildings which smelled musty, and I remember clearly the huge community bakery, with an entire wall of ovens, cast doors variously opening and closing on the steaming loaves.

Hira often used to take Edward and me to collect bread. I still remember the taste of it and the smell and nothing I have ever had since tasted so good. Edward and I once saw a knife fight break out in the bakery and Hira would not allow us to stay to watch.

I remember too the fig trees in the school yard, the nuns at school and in mass on Sunday and the well in the courtyard of our temporary but very grand home.

The well in particular sticks in my mind because Brandon dropped my two pet tortoises into it in order to prove that they were turtles. Why he could not have determined this with just one of the creatures in a bowl of water was not a matter I considered at the time, I was after all only six years old.

The singular and immediately obvious lack of swimming skills followed by an equally obvious inability to float established pretty quickly that they were not turtles. They might as well not have been witches. The frantic rescue attempts involving sticks with bent coat hangers proved fruitless for the well was deep and the tortoises, their classification no longer in debate, had quickly sunk to its depths in a manner one would expect of a stone - or a tortoise.

At the time I had a well-deserved reputation amongst my brothers for being a bit of a 'goody two shoes'. This was due no doubt in part to the fact that until then I was almost never in trouble, but probably also due to the fact that I often told tales on the other boys for their little transgressions, such as smoking, lighting fires in the outbuildings, or pinching cooking chocolate from the pantry and making white bread sandwiches; a sort of improvised 'pain au chocolat'. When we couldn't steal chocolate, we used sugar and white bread for a slightly less delicious treat. Sugar sandwiches were a real thing.

Brandon, as leader, and in common with most tyrants throughout history required total loyalty from his siblings. He considered me as something of a traitor and so had dubbed me a 'clecker-box', which was a common enough name for someone who told tales.

After we started school, we met and became friends with two local brothers; one named Mohammed the other named Ali. The boys did not attend the same school as us but were the sons of our maid Hira. Their father lived in France and they used to spend their holidays with him so it was not until school started that they came home and we all became acquainted.

As a result of that acquaintance and my reputation as a 'clecker-box', and for some reason unknown to me my nickname transformed from Clecker-box into 'Mohammed Ben-Clecker'. I have to admit that it had a certain originality and Arab authenticity to it, and even now I kind of like it. It beat 'thick head' and 'blubber guts' which were often used, sort of affectionately towards me. I was going to name this memoir 'Mohammed Ben-Clecker' but for reasons which will shortly become obvious, Father's Day suited better.

The nickname was first used when I told Hira about the drowning of the tortoises, and she told our father. Brandon received a lash or two with the belt as a result and, for some reason, though he had been unconnected with the misdemeanour, so had Will. It tended to be that way with our father; punishment was often handed out pretty indiscriminately. The important thing as far as our father was concerned was that justice had to be seen to be done, not necessarily to the right people, just seen to be done.

If a child got a whack, he did not deserve then it was OK, because he likely had in the past, or would in the future, escape a beating which he did deserve. In fact, our father had a theory which he happily and regularly espoused. He held that it was justified to thrash a child on sight due to the fact that it was either heading away from trouble or toward it. This, in the case of Brandon, Will and Edward, and to a lesser extent me, was almost certainly true, almost all of the time. Our young years, when not sleeping, were occupied with naughtiness and commensurate punishments when caught or suspected.

Brandon, along with Will, Edward, Mohammed and Ali had one day, as revenge for me telling our mother that the older boys were smoking, constructed a banner with the words 'Mohammed Ben-Clecker' painted on it. They paraded it in a line around the courtyard, stamping their feet and chanting 'Mohammed Ben-Clecker, Mohammed Ben-Clecker'.

Mohammed Ben-Clecker was not particularly worried about this, and to some extent I enjoyed the notoriety. Even our parents saw the funny side; peaceful protest in 1968 in Algeria it seemed was OK, at least in our courtyard if not elsewhere.

It's odd what the mind recalls from so long ago. For most things I guess there is no reason for the memory and it may be stimulated by a smell, by a sound or something else. For some memories however there is a more troubling cause.

Another of the few abiding memories of Algeria that I have, and I suppose shall have for the rest of my life, was of the library in the house we occupied. It's not a good memory and even now I am not sure what it means, I just know it makes me feel bad, it did at the time and it does now.

The library was vast. The floor was polished marble and cool, the high ceiling was supported with ornate white columns. Large, thin, white silk drapes hung from the walls. There was even an echo in the room, but not a single book.

My brothers and I would race around, skidding and sliding on the marble, an activity of which we never tired. It was more often than not far too hot to play in the courtyard and we were not allowed on the streets without Hira for reasons we were too young to understand. Huge ceiling fans turned day and night, forcing the air down over the floor and cooling the room with remarkable effect. We would often lie on the cool marble and sleep in the afternoons.

The reason I remember the library so well is however not to do with its vastness or its coolness or indeed any other physical characteristic. One afternoon Edward and I had been fighting in our bedroom. It was something all we brothers did daily with no ill consequence other than a black eye now and then or a bloodied nose, but this particular day we two combatants had disturbed our father.

Our mother was away in the UK at the time giving birth to our youngest brother so our father's drinking had been completely unchecked for several weeks. Ironically, without our mother his drinking, although uncontrolled, did not seem to cause the issues we witnessed when she was around.

A French woman named Claudette came to stay with us while our mother was away, she and Hira looked after us. I think Claudette was a family friend but can't remember much about her.

We would stay out of our father's way as best we could but occasionally his path and that of one of us would cross and then the sparks would fly but for a 6 or 7-year-old it was manageable.

On the day in question, he was not so much drunk as hung over and the noise from our little battle had woken him. He caught us both and dragged us by our collars into the library. He faced us off against each other and forced us to fight, which we reluctantly and unenthusiastically did.

It was the sort of thing you might see on an old black and white film, a method of parenting probably best left in the past. For example, if you catch your child smoking force him to smoke a carton of untipped Capstan or if he fights, put him in a ring. I get the antiquated he-man approach but I can't get the cruelty of it. My father was an intelligent and well-travelled man, what the fuck was he thinking? The humiliation and the guilt hurting my brother, the one I loved probably over all my other siblings… for what? If I fought him for my reasons, and I often did, all well and good but to do it on command, that really felt wrong.

I remember the awful unidentifiable feeling I had. Incredibly I never discussed it with Edward but I wonder did he feel it too. It was a sort of trepidation; not that I was going to get hurt or even that I would hurt him. I just knew it was wrong and feared where it would lead, or what it meant.

I was certainly not afraid of fighting, something which would always remain a characteristic of mine. I also was not in the least afraid of Edward. Although he was older, he lacked coordination or any fluidity in his movement. It was hard to identify but it was an awkwardness of movement, of flow. When stealing half pound bars of Cadbury chocolate from Lipton's supermarket in Haverfordwest several years later, he had exactly the same characteristic, which immediately alerted anyone to the nature of his activities.

Edward could be caught stealing even when he was not stealing, simply because he looked like he was about to. My other brothers and I used to refer to him as 'chronic', which really was not the correct word but perfectly suited our understanding of it.

The encounter in the library was not so physically gladiatorial as it sounds; there were no broken bones for example and there is only so much damage a 6 or 7-year-old and an 8 or 9-year-old can do to each other. Any damage done that day was not physical, and it was not done by Edward or by me, we were the reluctant protagonists. We just did not at the time realise the nature of it, or by whom it was caused or to whom.

Edward and I did not stop fighting each other on that day; we did however become pretty adept at fighting in silence. This was a peculiar and often hysterical skill, and one for which I and probably Edward, never found a useful alternative purpose, other than to avoid being detected by our father.

It would be unfair and inaccurate to characterise my father as just a man who drank too much and was cruel to his children. Our father, whom all my brothers and I respected and feared in pretty much equal measure, was a complicated man, a bag of extremes and of contradictions, but then who of us isn't a contradiction?

The extent of the love and respect we had for him far exceeded that which might have been afforded a 'normal' peaceful father, as did the extent of the fear. Perhaps one informed the other. As a starving man will enjoy a meal more than a moderately hungry man might, so will a child cherish the moments of kindness and fun. It is however an unfortunate but accurate observation made by Shakespeare that the evil that men do lives after them and the good is oft interred in their bones.

If anyone was to ask me in one word to sum up my feelings about my father it would be 'fear'. There is no question of that and I don't have to think about it, not for a second. I wish it were otherwise because I know my father was an extraordinary man and I know he was a good man. Perhaps the worst relic of my childhood is that very contradiction. I don't want to be confused. I just want things to be simple. Alas they are not.

Even now I still have bad dreams of him. It was so when I was 6, when I was 9 and it was the same many years after he died; though the fear subsided the memory of it has not. My father is probably the only thing that I have ever been afraid of.

This is not about fairness or unfairness to him; it is simply the truth. If the same person asked me to sum up, in only one word, the Atlantic Ocean, I would have said 'wet'. 'Wet', like 'fear' is accurate but is so woefully inadequate a description as to render it, for the purpose of understanding the Atlantic Ocean, meaningless. So, fear, whilst always my overriding feeling when remembering my father, does not fully explain who he was or the relationship I had with him, but it is the best I can do when limited to one word. It may have been different before Africa but I can't say as I don't have memories much before then.

Chapter Four

Father's Day
(1990)

This was a difficult chapter to write and it will be difficult to read, particularly if you have children. I have written it exactly as I remember it and in as much as it is painful, it does set a benchmark for our journey back to life. We did not need it, it did not remind us of how lucky we had been to have the life we had, because we always knew that. It did change us though and I do wonder what would have become of us if this had not happened... alas it did happen.

For what it cost we need not have bothered paying for a cabin on the boat to France because neither of the children slept due to their excitement, so, nor did we. Even breakfast seemed to be the most exciting adventure for them, and I was sure that if we had re-boarded the boat in Caen, and taken them home both the children would have revelled in having had such an adventure.

Lucy and I lived for the children and delighted at how their wonderment, pleasure and happiness was stimulated at every little thing, from the seagulls to the tomato ketchup sachets at breakfast; one of which they each were allowed to pocket for later snacks en-route. Look, speaking French already!

Father's Day

We had not taken a car to Europe before, and I was nervous about driving on the 'wrong side' of the road. Lucy point blank refused to get behind the wheel, which was odd because she's always been a far better driver than me, in fact it was she who taught me how to drive properly. We don't count the stolen cars in Ireland in the early eighties as 'driving', no one is at their best with the police in hot pursuit.

To be fair I made only one mistake on the trip south. It was after filling with fuel at a service station in the port, when I exited the garage forecourt and began to drive on the left, instead of the right side of the road. Lucy noticed and corrected me very swiftly. Fortunately, the roads were very quiet and the error helped to focus my mind for the remainder of the trip.

The journey from northern France was uneventful and reasonably smooth due to the excellent roads. En-route I regaled the children with promises of trips to the beach, swimming in the pool and barbecues, while Lucy steadfastly kept account of which side of the road the car was travelling.

Although we made good time, due to the inevitable toilet and sick breaks it was late Saturday afternoon when we arrived at the campsite just outside of the town of Royan. We checked in at reception and met up with Will, Karen and our nieces Marie and Kate and nephew Jake; they had arrived the day before. The cousins were as excited to see each other as they were to be on holiday.

After showing us the tent Will and Karen took the five children off to have a look around and to give us the chance to unpack the car.

The campsite was glorious. It was in a pine forest adjacent to the beach on the Côte Sauvage. That section of coast was covered in similar sites which were populated mostly with British and German tourists, but also many French who would come down from the cities for weekends.

The tent, which was huge, was located well away from others and had a parking area to the side, and a relatively private garden area to the front. It consisted of a main living and dining area, a kitchen space and three separate 'bedrooms' which were partitioned off with zip up canvas 'doors'.

The main bedroom had a double bed, the second room next to it had twin beds, and between the two rooms was a narrow space which constituted a fabric closet or hanging space. The smallest bedroom was given over to storage but the plan was to have Marie and Kate stay over one night when we had all settled.

The cooking area had an adequate stove and cooking rings, and there was a full-sized refrigerator, electric sockets and lights, a large plastic table and chairs and all the luxuries which would have amounted to 'glamping' had the concept been thought of at the time. Thankfully it had not been and the place was not therefore monstrously and inexplicably over expensive!

We brought a river of lemonade with us due to the expectation of high prices for soft drinks in France, and the enormous thirst of little children in warm weather. I stored five two litre bottles in the fridge and stacked several on the floor next to it with the remainder under the double bed. Lucy carefully stowed her beloved tea bags above the fridge in the neat fabric folder which acted as a pocketed shelf. She would never travel more than fifty yards from home without her Tetley tea bags, normally eight or nine per day would suffice. Lucy does like a cup of tea.

By the time we had unpacked and settled-in Will and Karen brought the children back, watered and fed, thanks to the onsite café. The children were bursting to use the pool, but exhausted and with promises of all day swimming the next day, we managed to get them off to bed by seven thirty.

Lucy cooked us a meal and was herself in bed by nine. Will called over shortly after with a bottle of wine and he and I sat up for an hour or so, before retiring ourselves. I was dead on my feet.

Before getting into bed, I quietly unzipped the children's section of the tent. Kirsty had kicked off her sheet and lay there in just her favourite cat patterned pants; her beautiful snow-white locks glued to her head with sweat. It was to be the hottest summer in thirty years in France. I folded the sheet down past her feet and gently kissed her on the forehead. I then kissed Eamon and whispered;

'Good night'. Neither of them stirred. I quietly resealed the zip to ensure no bugs could enter their 'room'. It was the last time I would ever kiss Kirsty, if I had known I would have climbed in next to her and cuddled her and kept her safe. What I wouldn't give for just one more cuddle, one more tantrum, one more anything, just one more moment with her?

I left the single nightlight on for the children, and too tired to find pyjamas, in my underpants I climbed into bed next to Lucy. It was about 11 o'clock on the 16th June 1990. It was the last day of the life we had known and had built together. Within four hours Kirsty would be dead and Eamon would be beginning an almost impossible fight for his life; a battle which would scar and change the three of us, irreparably and forever.

The first moment I knew something was wrong was at three thirty in the morning when Lucy woke me screaming. She was not trying to wake me; she was trying to get to the children. At first, I could not remember where I was, all around us was the whoosh of fire and the sound of aerosols bursting. The fire rolled across the ceiling above us in hungry inverted waves. Lucy had been on her feet on the bed and from her chest up she was surrounded in thick, acrid smoke. She collapsed just as I was regaining my senses. She was by now semi-conscious, stupefied with a combination of the smoke and the horror which surrounded us.

She had been trying to break through the burning wall of the closet which separated us from the children and which was by now full of burning clothes, which stuck to her arms as she fell.

Although still confused I knew it would only be a matter of seconds before we were all lost to the fumes and the flames. The situation was rapidly becoming hopeless. I'd been trained in fire rescue in the nuclear power station as part of my job and was aware of how fast the smoke and lack of oxygen would lead to muscle weakness and collapse. In training though you always know you are safe; this was very different.

I rolled backwards off the bed and dropped to the floor trying to get my bearings. I tried to breathe, it was hot and thick and it burned my throat, the air was almost void of oxygen so on my knees, staying as low as possible, I grabbed Lucy under her armpits and pulled her off the bed and began to struggle backwards.

The inner wall of the tent, which formed our 'bedroom' was already evaporating into ash as I reversed through it. My bum was on the ground by now and my back directed to the outer wall of the tent, just eight feet away but ablaze in a sheet of red. My legs pushing and slipping on the plastic ground sheet as I desperately dragged Lucy backwards with me, inch by dreadful inch.

Anything; any movement I could make to escape I made; I knew I could breach the burning wall; it was thin and disintegrating and although intensely hot I could easily break through it with my back and get out into the air; if I could just get that far.

I tried to breathe again and knew it was my last breath in the inferno, live or die, I knew we would at best get another 5 or 6 seconds of consciousness. The fire was greedily consuming every atom of oxygen, and if we did not get out now, we never would. My limbs were lead, and my lungs were empty… it surely was the end.

Lucy, semi-conscious could sense she had to work if she was going to live. She kicked and scrambled, her limbs flailing desperately but not aimlessly. I could feel her efforts and the force of her pushing back, ever closer to the wall and the air outside. Her feet slipped again and again on the ground sheet, like some cartoon of a character running backwards on the spot and about to take off. Mercifully the plastic ground sheet had not melted due to the gallons of lemonade which had melted and continued to leak in the incredible heat. Wading through melted plastic was a task we had inadvertently but mercifully been spared due to our efforts to economise.

At the very last of our efforts, the very limit, all but spent and ready to submit to the inevitable, we tumbled through the wall of the burning tent and gulped in the relative coolness of the air outside. We scrambled up the bank to escape the heat. When at a safe distance, still within the blanket of heat, both naked but for the remains of our burned underwear, I lay on top of my wife, too horrified to cry or to feel sorry for me or for her or for the children I said;

'They're gone Lucy but we're alive...

Even so many years later I cannot understand how or why the words came, all I know is that I said them and I meant them, and that she, my beautiful and destroyed wife had heard them. Maybe some auto-protect function of the human mind, I just don't know. It was the very worst and most unpleasant utterance I ever made or ever shall and the recollection of it, even decades later is painful almost beyond words.

I did not hear the scream, Lucy did;

'They're still alive Gav, I can hear them!' She could barely croak the words.

I had no idea if she had or had not heard anything but, in a moment, I was on my feet, I turned and ran back, back into the fire from which we had tumbled only moments before.

It wasn't brave or heroic, it was instinct; what else could any father do? As I ran towards it all I could see was flame, rising easily thirty feet into the air and catching on the overhanging pine branches and needles causing them to pop and screech, as though they too were screaming for rescue.

I guessed that if I ran fast enough, I could easily break through one side, run through the entire inferno and momentum alone would carry me through; it really did not seem so risky at the time. It was hopeless of course, nothing could have survived the inferno, but I had to try something... anything... I had to.

A few hours earlier we had removed the plastic table and 6 plastic chairs from the living area of the tent and stored them outside. Had we not the theory I had developed as I ran towards the fire, and in relation to my mass, and the momentum carrying me through, would have had a certain and fatal flaw. As it happens, at the time I had no memory of tables and chairs and detours around them would not have been a consideration anyway.

As I ran, naked but for my underpants, into what seemed to Lucy likely to be certain death I could hear her screaming for me to not go back. Later I learned that Will had arrived at that moment and thankfully stopped Lucy from following me.

I hit the outer wall of the tent at full pace, and went through it as though it was not there, I held my arm across my face to protect it. In two strides I was across the living area. I had thought my breath would last for the seconds required but it did not. I tried to breathe… and inhaled just dead heat. I staggered forwards through the inner tent and then tripped, I was in the children's section of the tent by now and could not even open my eyes; I tripped and fell forward directly into Eamon, my momentum carrying us both through the burning back wall of the tent.

I hit the ground outside the tent and began to gain my feet. I looked up and to my absolute gut-wrenching horror could see Eamon, my little boy, running, parallel to the burning tent instead of away from it. His hair was full ablaze, his pyjama's top and bottom were aflame; he was a living, running but silent human torch. I glimpsed hell on earth in that moment and the sight should have driven me mad, but it did not, not just then, just then my son needed me; the time for madness for Lucy and for me would come later.

In what felt an eternity but was only a moment I was on my feet and running after him just as Lucy rounded the corner of the back of the tent, and captured her beloved son in her arms. We both patted the flames out with our hands, afraid to hurt him and afraid not to extinguish them quickly.

There was no going in again and as sickeningly painful as it was to even contemplate, I knew that the obstacle over which I had tripped had been Kirsty's lifeless body.

So started the first day of our first holiday; the last day of our old lives, Sunday June 17th 1990; Father's Day.

Chapter Five

Meeting Lucy
(1984)

Given the awful experience I described in the previous chapter I think it would help now to tell you a little more about my wife. You know her name is Lucy so let me tell you how we met almost 40 years ago, and how we decided to give a relationship a try. It's a slight digression from the main point of the story, to which I shall shortly return, but a necessary one, I think.

Although I was born in the UK, I spent several years growing up in Ireland. By 1984 I was just 24 years old and had completed college in Limerick 9 months earlier. I'd managed a few months as a site engineer building an Atari factory in Limerick. Computer games apparently were about to become the next big thing.

The recession of the early eighties hit hard, and work was very scarce for everyone. Like so many Irish people before me, I got onto a boat heading for the UK. I was equipped with a £5 note, a bag, a degree in construction management and a £2000 student debt.

In spite of my roots in the UK it did not feel like I was returning home, it very definitely felt as though I was leaving.

Luckily, as mentioned, my brother Will lived in Gloucestershire so I was not homeless or destitute and he and Karen put me up for a few weeks until I found work. It would not be the last time they saved me with their kindness, but we shall come to that.

Reluctant to be a burden I sought and swiftly found employment which offered accommodation. As I'd worked in pubs in Ireland during my college years, I had little trouble getting such a job. That is how I arrived at the Swan Hotel in the beautiful Cotswold village of Bibury in March 1984.

The Swan was a quintessentially English country hotel, stone built with vines climbing its ancient walls. It was owned and managed by Mr Morgan, ably assisted by his gentleman friend Tim. Morgan was about 65-years of age and was an unashamed snob. He came from the world of hoteliers in London and had worked his way up whilst acquiring a self-belief, self-assurance and effortless condescension to everyone he encountered. In spite of this I liked them both, particularly Morgan and Morgan liked me. It was almost as if I, being such a rough diamond, did not require constant condescension. One tends to condescend only to those that matter, and that seemed to work for us both.

There was also the fact that I was very good at the job. In Ireland they take bar work seriously and I had 6 years' experience in good bars. Bar work had been good to me and paid most of my way through my college years. On several occasions Morgan noted my attendance to customers far exceeded their expectations and his. Whilst this often-attracted large tips from the well-heeled clients, it was clear that I took great pride in my work and did not seek such reward, though it was always welcome.

I was very quickly very happy at The Swan. It was a great relief to me to be self-sufficient with a base from which I could build. I had food, board and pay. I did not plan to stay working in a bar, even a very nice bar, but for now it served my needs handsomely.

On that first day Morgan welcomed me enthusiastically, and showed me around the hotel including the room where I was to stay. It was an attic room which was large enough in spite of most of it being of limited height. I was to share a bathroom immediately opposite my bedroom with the couple who lived in the room adjacent, the Head Chef and his wife, who was also a Chef.

Morgan explained that most of the staff shared a house in the village and that if I preferred, I might like to do that. I decided, before I went to bed that night that I probably would.

At the time I was still an avid, if a slow reader, and I had brought a few books with me to the UK. I had only one book left unread. I settled down and completed Thunderbolt and Lightfoot before going to sleep; it was a thin book which I'd already started.

A week earlier I'd finished a book by Robert Ludlum, one of my favourite authors. It was called *The Bourne Identity*; even now I wonder why it was not made into a film until 18 years later in 2002.

I awoke sometime in the early hours and made my way in the dark to the bathroom. I opened the door and as I fumbled for the light switch the light came on and through squinted eyes, I could see a very fat fellow and a small woman in the bed below.

'Wrong room, mate' said the fat fellow before turning off the light.

I stepped back out of the room muttering embarrassed apologies and pulled the door closed. Turning left I found the bathroom door and the light switch whereupon I emptied my bladder into the correct receptacle.

This would have been an insignificant event but for the fact that within fourteen months the woman I had almost met in the circumstance described above, stood, next to me, in a blue home-made dress, in Stroud Registry Office, saying

'I do'.

The following morning, I went down to familiarise myself with my new home and place of work. I met Bert, the old man who would each morning light the two log fires which sat under large stone mantels either side of the bar. Bert was a veteran of the Italian and other campaigns in World War Two. He'd fought one way or another from the outbreak until the end of the conflict. He was about seventy-five but looked ninety. He was tiny and had a stoop, and his broad West Country accent was difficult at first for me to understand.

Unlike so many real heroes of the time he was not in the least reluctant to talk about his experiences. In fact, he was relentless in tales of his exploits in amphibious vehicles, battle fields and the whore houses around Europe; with the sort of detail, one does not find in history books… thankfully.

Many of the staff found Bert boring and repetitive, and some were uncomfortable with his tales, but I enjoyed his company. I always gravitated towards older men and found they invariably had more to say than people of my own age. At the time many veterans were still around and the opportunities to hear first-hand accounts of such things were, to me, invaluable.

Bert would light the fires, and then sit at the bar where I would give him his free measure of dark rum, which was permitted by Morgan… along with the three extra measures permitted by me. It was unclear if Bert liked me, or just the rum but it didn't matter. He was a living, breathing - if a little racist -history, and it pleased me no end to see him totter out of the bar to his cottage, with the log fires blazing behind him.

The first time I saw Lucy properly, as opposed to an indistinguishable lump through squinted eyes, was the same morning I met Bert and heard of the German's ear he still had in his 'collection'. He'd offered to show me, but as much as I liked 'living history' I declined. He told me that it didn't look much like an ear anymore anyway.

By nine thirty all the staff, including kitchen, housekeeping etc. began to congregate in the dining room for breakfast. I was a little nervous as I

Father's Day

walked through the double doors into the large room, only to be greeted warmly and invited to join my new colleagues for breakfast. I remember that feeling of blind optimism which often inexplicably occupies the young and is gradually eroded as life experience is accumulated. Never underestimate what a friendly smile and a kind word can do for a person in a new and strange place.

There were about 10 staff sitting at two of the large round tables. Several asked me polite questions and exchanged other pleasantries as one does on such occasions, when a voice from the adjacent table asked;

'What part of Wales are you from?'

It was a surprise to me because I thought that my accent at the time was mostly Irish. Of course, it was not, I'd spent the last seven years there but mostly grew up in Wales. It was apparently also a surprise to everyone else at my table when the person spoke to a stranger who was not a customer. I learned later that it was unusual for Lucy to speak up about anything, and the staff thought it odd that she had. Her nickname was 'The Mouse'.

I responded stating that I was from South Wales; she replied;

'Me too, where about?'

Her voice was familiar, perhaps due to it having a very mild Welsh lilt. Since being back in the UK I had not spoken to any Welsh people. I replied telling her where I grew up but that I had lived in Ireland most recently. At this she either grew bored or reverted to her timid self and the conversation seemed to me to have ended. But then, without looking up she said;

'Did you find the bathroom?'

I blushed and realised only then that it had been she upon whom I had almost urinated. Clearly no one else knew what she was talking about and I was pleased that she and the fat man had not disclosed my embarrassing, though perfectly reasonable error.

She was a petite woman, five foot two at most. At the time I guessed her to be in her thirties; in fact, she was just twenty-five, a year and a bit older than me. She was dressed in a dowdy and modest fashion which aged her. Calf length thick woollen skirt, roll top jumper, heavy cardigan and large rimmed glasses. For all the world she looked like a librarian, or at least how I thought a librarian should look, I was twelve the last time I had visited a library so maybe things had changed.

Great Expectations, which I had borrowed when learning to read, had been destroyed. I recall that my mother would occasionally get a letter threatening a fine for it; so, I was terrified to go near the local library. Thus, I developed a fear of libraries I suppose. It didn't help that my eldest brother Brandon told me that I was going to be hanged for the offence - and I partly believed him. I was an exceptionally gullible child in many ways.

If this woman was a librarian, which was unlikely, she was not a scary librarian. Her hair was not greasy, but it seemed to stick to her face, as though to hide it. She looked down when she spoke, and seemed unsure of herself. She smoked three cigarettes during the twenty-minute breakfast, which for her consisted of several cups of tea and nothing else. I did not want to stare but once or twice during that breakfast she caught me looking at her; which I guess meant that she was looking at me.

After breakfast the staff helped clear up and I could not resist looking at her as she did her bit collecting plates; I was drawn to her, and had no idea why. I was impressed that she could carry so many plates in one arm, and I held the kitchen door open for her; as she passed, she lifted her head and smiled saying;

'Thank you',

It was the first time I had fully seen her face; it literally took my breath away; she had the most astonishingly beautiful smile I had ever seen, it started with her mouth but was completed in her eyes, which were velvet brown.

'Je vous en prie' I replied and immediately regretted it. I thought I'd come across like some sort of wannabe gigolo.

There was something else there in her face though; her smile was real, no one could fake that, but there was something beneath it, something it was difficult to define but the closest I could come was 'resignation', acceptance of one's lot in life, *no expectation*. I supposed that she did not use her beautiful smile every day.

I hoped that our paths would cross again in the course of work and I was not disappointed. Adjacent and almost an annex to the bar with only the spirits store room and a short corridor between was the lunch bar. This was an exceptionally popular early afternoon haunt for visitors to the village and for the well-heeled locals. One of Lucy 's duties was to stock and run the snack bar and this entailed having to visit my bar to pick up drinks for her clients. She would also sometimes come behind the bar and help herself when I was too busy to serve her.

As a consequence of our roles, she and I had daily contact and we rapidly grew to know one another. Apart from both being from South Wales we learned that, by remarkable coincidence, our respective maternal grandfathers had worked together in the health service in South Wales. Her grandfather trained one of my uncles and a cousin for a time. We also both came from large obsessively religious families, though on the opposite ends of the Christian spectrum.

Lucy 's husband at the time, who was the head chef, was ultra-cautious of any relationships she had, and would make numerous visits to the bar and the lunch bar under the most implausible excuses to check up on her. This was not because of me; it had apparently always been that way.

Gradually I could see the sort of relationship they had, though she, for the most part tried to conceal it. It soon became evident that her husband would not trust her even to go to the local shops

Father's Day

without going to extraordinary lengths to keep tabs on her. He checked the mileage on the car for example if she had to drive into Cirencester, and he would only ever allow her a small allowance from her own wages - even her tips went into his bank account. It was 1984 and the notion of controlling and coercive behaviour was unheard of, though to be fair, the physical abuse was obvious to most.

It was obvious also that everyone in the hotel knew of the terrible time she had with her husband, but no one really seemed to care. It was overlooked by Morgan and Tim because they preferred a smooth-running ship, regardless of what was going on, and besides, both Lucy and her husband were excellent chefs, neither of whom they could afford to lose.

Of all the times her husband had unexpectedly entered either of the bars, all he found was us talking and often laughing. He hated it though. We had nothing to hide because we did not think about each other in any way we should not, though we were becoming very close, it was wholly innocent and platonic.

Bibury was a little out of the way, and quite soon after I arrived Lucy suggested that I find myself a girlfriend with a car. By coincidence and unbeknown to her I had a blind date that evening with a nurse called Steph, who happened to have a car; a VW Beetle. The following day I announced to her that I had taken her advice and had indeed found a girlfriend with a car. She guessed the truth, but seemed quite sad at the news, which was in contrast to how her husband received it. She tried to hide it but it was very obvious to me. I thought no more of it though. I was content with Steph and her Beetle and together we made lots of trips into Oxford, Cirencester and other places.

On several occasions I commented to Lucy on how she dressed, she was OK with that and I knew she would be. One afternoon she'd escaped into Cirencester and bought some new clothes more fitting for a 25-year-old. The fat man stopped her wearing them and gave her a very hard time regards why she wanted to 'look like a slut'.

What I was to discover, only later, was that Lucy had started to stand up for herself, in small ways at first, but over the space of just three weeks she had started to fight back against the oppression and bullying she had endured since she met the fat man, when she was aged just fifteen.

To me, she seemed content to have someone with whom she could talk and confide, and I was happy to be that person. I disliked her husband but knew her relationship was not my business, not yet anyway. I still had firm plans on marrying some Irish Catholic virgin, preferably with larger breasts than Lucy, though hers were more than adequate from what I could see through the layers of cardigan and blouse.

The change in things happened one night when all the hotel employees went out together for a Chinese meal in Cirencester. There were about twenty of us in all. Lucy sat on the left of the fat man and I was on his right. We'd all been to a bar beforehand and spirits were high. Several of the staff made jokes and uncharacteristically Lucy proffered a humorous anecdote of her own. It was not particularly funny but everyone could see the effort she had made and they laughed anyway, everyone that was except for her husband, who without looking at her and through a full mouth grunted;

'That's stupid; you're naff at telling jokes'.

The whole table fell silent, which doubled her humiliation and I remember feeling desperately bad for her, as I presume did everyone else.

Lucy made her excuses and headed to the bathroom; a couple of others followed in the usual fashion. I wondered if she was upset or embarrassed. The fat man kept on eating, reminding me of Mr Creosote and a 'wafer thin mint'.

When she returned to the table, Lucy looked at me from across the room and not caring who saw, she smiled her wildly beautiful smile and did not conceal it. As she sat down, we both reached and briefly touched hands behind the fat man. I had never before or since felt such a feeling of optimism as I did in that moment, and I still cannot fathom why. Some things concerning the heart defy explanation, I guess.

Lucy and the fat man had arranged a week away in Portsmouth, so the next morning she needed to go into Cirencester to collect some essentials. An unusual non escorted trip made all the more unusual when she offered to take me into town, and he did not object. Staff with cars lifting staff without cars into town was common enough, and Steph was on duty in John Radcliffe Hospital in Oxford, so her VW Beetle was out of reach that day.

I do not believe in love at first sight, who in their right mind does? Love after second or maybe third sight though is maybe another matter. Even after thirty-nine years of being married to her I can't say exactly when I fell in love with Lucy; it doesn't really matter I suppose. Maybe it was the evening in the restaurant when our fingertips touched, literally behind the fat man's back, as he fought over the next rib, maybe before that or after.

If I had to bet on it though, I would put my money on it being when we had driven into Cirencester that day and just after she had picked up the items the fat man needed for the holiday. She'd bought me a mint choc chip ice-cream; we were looking through a shop window at men's shoes when she gently slipped her arm into mine and kissed me on my neck.

I maybe loved her before that kiss, but for sure I loved her and no other from that moment, for the rest of my life. Having not yet lived the rest of my life at this moment I suppose I cannot know for sure but I guess it will be so. We stopped at my place on the way back and made love, embarrassed, shy, intense and perfect.

She'd gone that afternoon for their holiday, and I barely slept the whole time she was away;

something unusual for me. I wondered if the quick and intense passion we had shared would still be there when she got back. As the days went by the doubt and uncertainty grew. Steph noticed I was distracted. She'd asked why I was aloof and threatened to dump me. The less bothered I seemed about the threats the more intense she became. It was a blessing that she worked in Oxford and nobody had yet invented texting. I felt bad for her for a time; she was a nice girl and the only girlfriend on whom I ever cheated.

It was a Thursday afternoon when Lucy came into the bar. She looked different, she'd had her hair cut, it was to just above shoulders and showed off her fantastic, elegant neck, but it was more. Although clearly nervous there was also a confidence, a self-belief I had not seen before and I loved it. I knew for absolutely sure that I loved her; it had physically hurt while she was away, not just the uncertainty, but the hopelessness of this turning out in any way successful. What were the odds?

I knew there was so much more to know; that I was unwrapping something special, someone special who had been cocooned in pain and misery for most of her life. She was a beautiful, nervous, courageous miracle whose path was meant to cross mine. She approached the bar;

'Hi, could you let me have forty B and H Gav?' I was unsure as I passed the cigarettes to her and took the money, holding it in her hand for a moment longer than necessary.

'Nothing's changed?' I asked.

She smiled her, big, big smile and my heart leapt.

'I haven't even unpacked and I am here pretending I need cigarettes, what do you think?'

I took her hand and put it on my chest so she could feel my heart beating against my ribs and she laughed;

'Don't have a heart attack.'

With that the door to the bar opened and in came the fat man, clearly searching for his errant wife-servant.

'There you are… I thought you were getting fags' he gasped having just managed the stairs down to the bar.

He didn't acknowledge me, he just turned as she waved the two packs of twenty in his direction and she began to obediently follow;

'We need to talk properly' she whispered as she left.

It was a couple of days before we got the chance to talk. The fat man had gone to play golf with a friend, and Lucy was covering in the kitchens. She came into the bar and ordered a gin and tonic, which for her was odd as she did not normally drink.

It was early and the place was empty but for us. She sat on the stool at the end of the bar with her back to the log fire. She had an envelope under her hand and I, after serving her drink, placed my hand on hers. She pulled it away, I looked at her; there was no smile. My heart sank and I wondered what it could be. I was as certain of her feelings for me as I was of mine for her.

'You need to know about me before this goes any further' she said quietly, not looking at me.

'You're not married are you' I laughed.

There was a flicker of a smile which she suppressed before it could grow.

'I know that I love you Lucy' I said. I'd felt it but had not said it before. A tear broke from the corner of her eye and rolled down her cheek. My heart was in my mouth.

'I love you too, but you need to read this.'

She thrust the letter into my hand. 'I'm not what you think; you deserve someone nice, not me… I am not what you think I am.'

I was beyond confused and lamely tried to joke 'Well I know you definitely haven't got a cock!'

'Just read it' she said, it explains… 'I'll come back down in an hour and we can talk.'

Reluctantly I agreed and she left, drying her eyes as she walked.

It was a thin letter and before I started reading it, I wondered all sorts of things from terminal illness to her being some sort of criminal. I opened the envelope and began reading; even her hand writing was exquisite. When I finished reading the overwhelming feeling, I had was one of surprise, not of pity or anything else I can remember.

She had explained, almost in clinical terms and without the least hint of self-pity but simply as a chronicle of the facts of how at the age of fourteen she had been drinking cider with her sister Jen in

LLangattock and ended up being assaulted by a group of motorbikers. No unnecessary details or emotive language, just the facts, as I now relay them, with her permission, to you. She had added an apology for not telling me before things had gone so far.

She had been fourteen years old and her life had from that moment, and for the last 10 years, been a torment. She wrote how she attached herself to the fat man from the age of fifteen, and that he had been the only person she had ever told and he had used it to control her. How she had suffered Bulimia for most of those years and continued to fight it, but also welcome it, as a means of survival through the nightmare she lived each day.

It was clear from her writing that she was highly intelligent and self-aware and knew that she had allowed this subjugation because she felt unworthy, unclean, but now she did not feel that.

She explained the turmoil she felt over the possibility of spoiling my life and her guilt at cheating, and wanting me, but it was time she did something just for her.

It was unchartered territory for me but how she could think anyone would infer anything adverse about such a dreadful experience was beyond me. The complexities of such an experience I am now of course more familiar with, and understand more, in so far as any man can, and maybe I was being simplistic but that was how it was. I really didn't care about her past, whatever it was.

Father's Day

When she came into the bar an hour later it was clear that she was not the distressed, vulnerable woman she was entitled to be. She could be abused and bullied and controlled, but she held onto herself, and it was that which she had given to me, the most valuable thing she had. Of course, it was a front and she was terrified for a few moments but she did not show it. This was not a person looking for sympathy or effect; she loathed self-pity and was incapable of it. She simply needed to dispose of a truth now, before anything more developed between us.

I did not approach her and did not try to put my arms around her. I wanted to but it was not what she wanted, and I could see that. I handed the letter to her and said;

'Bugger, you've been through the wars, haven't you?' It was the best I could do. 'I'm kind of flattered that you chose me to tell before anyone else' I continued, unsure 'except for the fat man.'

Then there it was… back for sure, her beautiful smile;

'I was under anaesthetic when I told him' She laughed. 'I didn't know how to tell you and there was no morphine handy' she continued; 'It's a bit of a conversation killer'

I put my hands on hers and she stopped.

'Don't' she said. 'Don't be nice, it'll make me cry and I hate crying'. She smiled and sniffed.

'Do you want to talk about it' I asked.

'Not yet' she replied quietly, 'But soon, I want to, I've never wanted to before but I want to now'.

'We've got forever' I said and I kissed her on her lips. Tears continued to roll down her cheeks unabated, I could taste them in our kiss.

'I'm leaving him' she said.

I was surprised but pleased, and sort of not really surprised after all when I thought about it;

'When?' I asked.

'In about forty minutes.' she nervously laughed.

I was amazed as she relayed to me what she had done while on holiday. She had written three letters, one to me, one to the fat man, and one to the fat man's family. The letter to me I had read. The letter to the fat man was eight pages long and I did not ask to see it, it was not for me and I had no interest in it whatsoever.

She explained that it catalogued his brutality and his treatment of her over the years and informed him that she was leaving. It also contained a copy of the letter she had written to his family, which also was eight pages long, and which would be sent to them if he tried to stop her leaving, or contested the divorce she was about to initiate. She explained to me that my reaction to her letter was more than she had hoped for, but she had decided to leave regardless of what my reaction was.

Within thirty minutes her mother arrived to collect her. We made our goodbyes politely and no agreements or arrangements between us were made, they were unspoken.

That evening the fat man burst into the bar demanding to hear what I knew. I feigned innocence and a complete lack of any knowledge of the matter and he believed me, or did not, I really didn't care.

Lucy and I kept in touch daily by phone, she at her parent's house in Crickhowell and me from the public telephone box opposite my accommodation in Bibury. By August things were becoming difficult for me at The Swan. Over the weeks I learned more and more of the torture Lucy had endured and it was all I could do to contain my anger. I was not expecting any problems, men who mistreat women in such a way as he had Lucy are rarely a risk to real men, but the fat man had hit the bottle heavily, and without a loyal wife-servant to cover his regular drunk days, he was in danger of losing his job.

Morgan saw me as the architect of all the disruption. I had arrived and upset the happy little ship. That Lucy endured such unhappiness daily was not a consideration for him. For some reason Morgan felt it was his job to interrogate me about Lucy's whereabouts and intentions, and my offer to resign was welcomed by him in the third week of September and even rewarded with a full month's pay.

It was a time which suited me. Lucy had applied for one job when she had settled in South Wales; it was managing four hire shops in Cardiff. She was shortlisted out of eighty applicants and given the job without a second interview. Clearly, I was not the only person who found her impressive. Within a month she had a flat in the city and in

September I moved in with her. I found work in the Cedars Hotel, in the city and there began our adventure together; an adventure which thirty-nine years later continues.

I anticipated some awkwardness from my parents over my choice of wife but not the cruel and utterly unrelenting dogma they displayed; we have covered much of that, I think.

I took Lucy to Dursley to meet my mother who had flown over from Ireland to see my brother Will. She refused to meet her when she discovered she was separated, and possibly worse, a Protestant. This rather set the tone and when a week later we visited my grandmother and maiden aunt Esta, my aunt had suggested over lunch that it was;

'Surprising what one can find in the gutter'. She considered herself quite clever. Thirty years later Lucy surprised her, and many other relatives, with the depth of love and care she (and others) showed the old woman until her death. More astonishing was the fact that Lucy never liked her, but would not allow that to change the fact that she could be kind to her.

I had wanted to tell everyone in the family Lucy's full story, to tell them of the cruel torment that she had suffered, but she forbade it. She really was indifferent to what others thought, and cared only what I thought. Many people claim indifference but to meet Lucy is to know its true meaning. She was quite incapable of a hard thought or hatred for anyone or anything, she remains so to this day. It is a fine quality and I admire it greatly. I feel sad for those who do not see it, or perhaps claim not to so as to conceal their own failings.

As every day passed, she amazed me more and more with her stoicism and forthright approach to all things, but most of all with her absolute contentment. That she was so inspirational, so incredible a human being made the rejection from my parents all the more bitter. Not for my loss, I had lost nothing, it was for theirs but they would never know it.

So now you know a little about Lucy and how we met. We'd spent only a few months in Cardiff before I secured a job as a Quality Inspector with TI Creda near Bristol. We married in May 1985 and Eamon, our son, was born in the August, on the feast of the Assumption which must have really hacked my parents off.

We rented a small house in Dursley near to my brother Will and later I managed to get a job in Berkeley Nuclear Power Station. By 1987, after being transferred we were living in North Wales and along came our daughter Kirsty, at just under 5 pounds in weight and no longer than my wrist watch.

That I suppose brings us rather neatly back to 1990 and to Father's Day. The year Lucy and I thought was going to be good for us, the year we took a holiday. It is where we left you dear reader, in the last chapter.

Chapter Six

No Hope
(June 1990)

Within moments of the utter, bottomless despair, the loss of all hope for the children, both of us felt immeasurable elation, and guilt, and fear, and dread, and confusion.

No one who had witnessed the fire would have supposed anyone could have escaped its grasp. That we three had done so was a wonder. I had never felt such a moment of joy and of hope as I did when Eamon came out of the flames, insane joy, borne of unfathomable despair. Not as uncommon bedfellows as one might suppose. He was gone and yet he was back. I don't mean to sound biblical, but it was what it was.

Other holiday makers were by now gathered, some with tiny fire extinguishers, unable to get close enough for them to reach the flames with their jets. I lifted Eamon into my arms, and followed a woman into her chalet where there was a bath. Eamon was so badly burned that conventional advice on how to treat him was meaningless, he needed water and lots of it, and fast.

He was black, almost all of his hair was missing and a large swathe of his body had already begun to leak essential fluids and blood, colouring the black in some sick mosaic.

What can a human mind take? What can it see, experience, bury and re-live without insanity descending upon it, infesting it to destruction?

Surely this had to be the limit? All I could concentrate on now was my son and keeping him alive long enough for ambulances and experts to arrive. They'd save him... right?

I immersed him waist deep into the half-filled bath and gently dropped the cooling water over what I supposed were his pyjama's, but were the scorched remnants of skin over exposed flesh. The woman whose chalet we had invaded, in turn, poured cold water over my raw back in an effort to dull the pain, which had until that point been suppressed, I assume by adrenalin.

Eamon was calm, he didn't cry, he stared ahead and recited nursery rhymes with me while Lucy, more seriously burned than me, ran around the tent's remains screaming hysterically for her daughter.

I knew I only had moments left with my little boy, and I determined to make them as pleasant as the circumstances would allow. I told him how the next day he would be on the beach and finding crabs, and eating ice-cream with his sister. I lied and lied and lied to him.

Eamon began to shake, his beautiful brown eyes widened and his calmness seemed to be replaced with fear, the end was close and it destroyed me again and again. Even now as I try to write this account, the pain of his suffering is almost completely unbearable. That moment cast me for the entire of the rest of my life, my love for my son was accompanied and equalled right then by an utter and irrational hatred of everything else on earth, and in the heavens, of everyone who has ever complained about anything less than this. Here was my child de-vested, in shock and in pain and a moment from death and looking for nothing but an ice cream on the beach the next day with his sister.

The emergency services arrived after almost an hour and within minutes Eamon, Lucy and I were in separate ambulances heading for Royan. Lucy was in the lead ambulance, Eamon in the second and I was in the last. Pascal, the paramedic administered morphine to me as I lay on my tummy, my back having been burned by the walls of the tent.

I closed my eyes and begged that I somehow could be awoken from the nightmare still unfolding. There was to be no respite, and as if the gods and demons who designed this path for their amusement had heard my pleas, the ambulance slowed, and balancing on my chin I could see out of the vehicle's front window.

The ambulance in front was pulling off the highway onto the shoulder. My ambulance followed. The driver's door and then the rear doors of Eamon's ambulance opened, and in the back, I could clearly see the paramedics in the unmistakeable and desperate act of CPR. Moments dragged in agonising anticipation but then the doors closed again and the ambulance took off at high speed. It could only mean that Eamon was still holding on, why otherwise would they rush? I prayed, out loud, I swore and cursed God and then begged him to save my child. Eamon's ambulance stopped again… and again the doors flew open and again the paramedics carried out CPR, and again the doors closed and it sped off at high speed, with my ambulance in pursuit.

As we approached an intersection Eamon's ambulance peeled off and mine carried on. As though to anticipate the conclusion I would have drawn Pascal explained that Eamon was going direct to the burns unit in Bordeaux while Lucy and I were going to another closer hospital.

Was this an answer to my prayers? Was it maybe just one card in our favour? I did not know at the time that Hôpital Pellegrin in Bordeaux was possibly Europe's leading burns unit and Eamon would be there in less than thirty minutes, if he could hang on. Maybe… maybe, just the thinnest of luck had shifted our way.

Lucy and I arrived in the local hospital; we were seen and immediately put back on two ambulances and taken to Bordeaux. Various staff had heated exchanges with the paramedics but we did not know why. I presume they took us to a regional hospital in Royan not equipped to deal with our injuries. I have little memory of the journey to Bordeaux from the first hospital thanks in part, I assume, to Pascal's enthusiastic administration of morphine.

I do have a vague recollection of being on my belly on a table surrounded by people. I had arrived early in the morning, stupefied from morphine and was taken to theatre where my burnt skin was scrubbed off and I was covered in cream and bandaged. It seemed to me that the surgeon was being very rough, and I tried in my best French to explain that it had been an accident; it had not been our fault. I don't know why I felt the need to explain but I did; Catholic up-bringing perhaps, that ever-present rucksack of guilt, carried for life. I felt they were being rough to punish me. I later supposed the cruelty had been in my imagination but have never been sure.

Ironically, I sort of relished the excruciating pain however and offered it in my mind to my son, who by now could be alive or dead for all I knew. I kept asking the staff about him and they would not answer, perhaps they did not know, or maybe it was my appalling French.

I awoke properly some hours later in the Intensive Care Unit of the Bordeaux hospital, confused and disorientated, it was still Sunday June 17th 1990, it was still Father's Day.

There was no moment of thinking everything was OK, no momentary release as one often hears related by people suffering trauma. I knew in an instant what had happened, it was seared into my mind and would form the stuff of my nightmares, sleeping and waking for years to come; initially constant and unrelenting but eventually occasional, but always the same, never tolerable, never welcome, just thankfully less and less frequent.

Father's Day

When I woke, I could see Lucy in the bed opposite, she was sitting up. We had our own little room in the Intensive Care Unit. My heart broke for her, just as I know hers did for me. She was bandaged, all of her arms, her head and most of her torso. I tried to smile at her.

'Your brother saw my tits' she said.

She was referring to the fact that she had only her pants on when the fire occurred and modesty, normally utmost in her mind, was the furthest thing from it. Incredibly I laughed, we both did. Maybe normality, humanity had not completely abandoned us after all.

I tried to sit up and struggled, my arms and back were on fire, they were burnt and although relatively insignificant burns compared to Eamon, they were very painful. The acrid stink of burned hair filled my nostrils still, and my hands were still blackened. It's not how one imagines it to be in hospital but it is how it is. I did not smell bleach and disinfectant I smelt fire and smoke.

A tube was attached to my arm and without thinking I pulled it out, I tried to get out of bed and a nurse rushed in to stop me. The nurses had so far refused to tell Lucy about Eamon. They were the enemy; everyone was the enemy to me at that time. I know it's wrong and unfair but I didn't care, I still don't. We'd brought our family to France and the French had killed our daughter, and they would not tell me about my son. The French were the enemy, France was the enemy; everyone was the enemy. I wanted my daughter, I wanted Kirsty.

Lucy, not normally given to extremes, added her reasonable but determined requests to my apparently unreasonable demands to have news of Eamon. If he was dead, we needed to know. The nurse would not confirm anything until a doctor entered the room. It was fortunate that her English was poor and did not extend to the extensive resource of abusive expletives at my disposal, all of which I used, repeatedly and vigorously.

The doctor it seemed understood perfectly and was, probably partly in reciprocation, very direct and informed us that Eamon was still alive and within a deep Intensive Care Unit or 'ICU' within the ICU itself but unlikely to survive. He explained that we could not see him.

We both assumed that he was lying, we thought that they were afraid to break the news to us so we demanded to see him. Eventually the doctor agreed that in the evening, after his dressings, we would be allowed to see our son.

It took upwards of 10 minutes for us to scrub and gown up and then to enter a small glass room where we had to put on another gown, head coverings and masks. Both of us were pushing along drips on tripods with tubes attached to our arms and we must have looked like casualties from World War One; we felt black and white and grainy and doomed.

Eventually we were led into another room. Double gowned nurses with masks looked on, and could not hide the tragedy in their eyes above their masks. Some things I guess, humans never get used to. In the room, which resembled a square glass box, was a bank of machines in a semicircle. A large rubber ball inflated and deflated. In the centre was a bed and on the bed was our beloved son. Insanely inappropriately I thought of the Monty Python machine that famously went 'Beep' and wondered which one it was for they all emitted one sound or another, presumably indicating all is well… for now.

Eamon was bandaged from head to foot, with a slit for the mouth and one each for his eyes. He looked like a fat, small mummy. He was hugely swollen with oedema. Tubes ran from his mouth and his body into the machines. His head was at least double its normal size and fluid, presumably a mix of his own bodily fluids and applied creams seemed to seep from most of the bandages. His little chest rose and fell in sync with the rubber ball.

Lucy fainted out cold at the sight and hit her head against the door as she fell. Two nurses helped her to her feet, but she would not go back to bed until she had seen Eamon properly, and told him she was there.

We could not touch him and he was deep in an induced coma. I asked the doctor in charge what the prognosis was, and requested that the news not be sugar coated. The Doctor obliged and explained that Eamon could not hear us and that he was not likely to live for more than a few hours. He was apparently by far the most extensively burned patient they had ever had to treat. He explained that most people with flesh deep burns over more than forty percent lasted a few weeks at best. Eamon was estimated to have over eighty five percent total depth third degree burns.

They planned to keep him in an induced coma for as long as he could survive. He told us that Eamon was not going to regain consciousness for us to say goodbye. They expected full renal failure imminently, he was already on respiratory support and the likelihood of infection killing him was not just high, it was a virtual certainty. He explained that Eamon had had heart failure twice en-route, something I already knew, and once on the operating table;

'He has a five per cent chance at best'. Realising that perhaps he had been a little too direct he added;

'In his favour he is very young and the younger burn victims are the better the chances are'

For some reason I felt compelled to offer that Eamon had been breast fed, thus was very healthy. Rules of normal engagement were suspended; the doctor would understand what I meant… or he would not.

Lucy and I spent 10 days in the ICU, during which time there was no improvement in Eamon's condition. Our relationship with the staff had not improved by the fourth day and it seemed to us that we were being treated as though somehow the accident was our fault. This all changed when the police arrived on the Wednesday or Thursday and interviewed us both, separately and at length, while we were still in the Intensive Care Unit.

A British consular officer appropriately gowned and masked and a doctor, one I had not previously met, were present for the interviews and it was all exceedingly formal. The doctor was not overtly unkind but he was the least sympathetic and it showed.

I was quizzed extensively about various issues including the apparently large amount of exploded lemonade bottles. They asked me where we had stored aerosols and what they were. I told them that these had been anti bug sprays, and other innocent products and that they had been stored above the fridge in a material storage unit. I suggested to them that exploding aerosols were probably what woke Lucy in the first place.

The mention of the location of the aerosols seemed to strike a chord with the men and they nodded understanding. I did not know at the time that the fire had started in the fridge just under the tins and was due to an electrical fault in the fridge.

The consular officer explained that a Judge had been appointed to head an investigation which would take many weeks but the police were authorised to give their preliminary report informally. He later explained that the procedure in France was very formal but also very leaky and most people would be aware of the conclusions, sometimes months before they were made official.

The officers expressed their condolences and wished me 'bon chance' for Eamon. The older officer, assuring me of his prayers and those of his family, which I was surprised to find deeply moving, he clearly meant it.

The consular officer apologised for the intrusion and assured me that replacement passports and documents were being arranged and that he would visit again soon.

I disrobed and started back to our room but a nurse approached telling me that we had visitors. I was guided directly to yet another gowning area where I was helped on with another gown and mask. It seemed odd to gown up when leaving the ICU but I followed instructions, keen to see who was visiting. We had had no contact with anyone for several days.

I was still extremely sore and found it hard to move, having to push the tripod around was awkward and cumbersome and all the robing and disrobing was an annoyance, everything was an annoyance.

As I prepared Lucy came into the room, accompanied by a nurse. The nurse smiled warmly at me, something she had not done before or maybe she had, and I was getting better at seeing smiles behind masks. Lucy was pushing her own drip on its tripod. She smiled at me, a sad smile, even sad her smile still reached me in the deepest places.

'How do I look?' she said.

Lucy had never worn make up in her life but I joked:

'You could cut down on the blusher but otherwise beautiful'.

Father's Day

I felt so sorry for her, how could she possibly bear this burden? I knew that once in her life she had already suffered beyond what any person should endure. Her regular nightmares for our first few years together had been testament to that. She'd wake screaming hysterically, arms flailing, until I could wrap myself around her, and bring her back to us, our home, our life and the knowledge that no more bad things would happen. I'd lied; I could not keep the bad things away, not from her or from our children. Now, here again, here was catastrophe visiting her and as usual, she was behaving like the remarkable being that I knew her to be from the day I had taken the mint choc chip ice-cream from her in Cirencester and she had kissed my neck, while I was looking at shoes and later, I had told her I loved her and meant it and always would.

Self-pity was a concept she simply would never entertain and I admired and continue to admire that rare quality in her above all others, even above her fantastic but now moderately scorched breasts.

We had no idea who would be visiting us. Consideration of how our disaster would inevitably affect others was not a high priority, not even a consideration at that point. I was oblivious also to the fact that I had been sedated since the accident and my judgement had not been entirely my own, neither of us knew what day it was.

The door opened into a large white room with a red horizontal line painted around its entire perimeter, plastic chairs were neatly lined up each side. The light was much brighter than in the ICU, hurting our eyes for a moment and making it hard to see who was there. Sitting down one side were three of my brothers, Will, Brandon, the eldest and Edward. On the other side were my parents and my sister Leonora and Lucy's parents. All of them were gowned in blue disposable gowns and masked in white surgical masks. I was unsure if it was for their protection or ours.

It struck me that this was the most of my family I had seen together for several years, in fact since about 1978, when we were all last in one place at the same time. Only Mike the youngest, and Roger were missing. It was also the first time our 'in-laws' had met.

In contrast to the abandonment we had received from my parents, Lucy's parents had always been loving and supportive of our relationship, and very much a part of the children's lives. The loss to them must have been unbearable.

My father approached me and I put my arms around him; he, uncomfortable with the only embrace we had ever had and ever would share patted me on the back inadvertently causing excruciating pain as he said;

'Pull yourself together'.

He did not say it unkindly and I did not take it so. It was just the way it was. At least they had come. It had taken the death of one child and the near death of the other to make them re-evaluate their position, but such thoughts were pushed to

Father's Day

the back of my mind, for now, but not totally out of it.

My mother put her arms around 'Soiled Goods'. It was not a time to wonder or to hold bad feelings, the situation was tragic for everyone. She promptly enquired as to Eamon's status in terms of Catholic baptism and we simply agreed to her suggestion that a priest visit to carry out baptism and extreme unction, regardless of the risk of infection. We were just too exhausted to fight. As I observed in the first chapter, entry into and exit from the world of Catholics apparently requires some ritual, preferably in Latin. We later however asked the staff to prohibit any priests, witch doctors or Voodoo practitioners.

Upon hearing how each of the family members had heard the news we both felt great pity for them all. My parents for example were in Church in Ireland on the Sunday morning and my eldest brother Brandon had taken a call from Will and gone to find them. It cannot have been easy for them… any of them.

It's an odd thing but in many ways, relations informed of tragedy and not close to it or directly involved suffer a particular type of grief, shock or ordeal; hopelessness I suppose. I have said this to others and no one ever seems to get what I mean. It's as if they think that to allow consideration of those feelings of others, somehow would diminish the pity we 'deserve', because we must hurt the most. It doesn't work like that… there is a point at which grief and pain exceeds meaningful measure or comparison, and we all, all of us, were in that region of pain…. together. Lucy and I have always seen it this way, even if people do not believe that, or do not understand it.

I know the accident and the loss of Kirsty profoundly and irrevocably hurt my brother Will and Karen, my sister-in-law… and the cousins too. We were very close, and they actually witnessed the events first hand. I often feel guilty that it was Lucy and me who were the focus of so much kindness and sympathy, perhaps at the exclusion of their feelings. The fact is that they suffered every bit as much as we did. Ironically, I know they will not endow us with such consideration… it is there none the less. Over the coming years too their selfless support for us and for Eamon in his recovery was immediately and costly to them in many ways, but hugely helpful to us as a family. Of course, later we did what we could to compensate them financially; that was all we could do. Money hardly seems enough in such circumstances I suppose, no matter how significant an amount.

I also often imagine how awful it must have been for Brandon bringing my parents out of church to tell them their grandchild was dead. In a way being there, at the accident, is a distraction from the reality. I don't suppose many readers will understand this but I know many victims will.

I say this with all sincerity and whilst my parents had behaved badly to us for years, they were still people and in their own way and perhaps due in part to that behaviour, the whole thing must have been very difficult for them. No rational person wishes pain on another and I did feel deeply for their pain, as did Lucy. It did not, and does not change what they did to us, to her.

A few years after the accident I was working in Bristol and a colleague whose wife had left him and taken the children was having a bit of a moan about it. I, like other colleagues listened sympathetically and then he said, as if he had some realisation;

'God sorry Gavin, here I am going on about a divorce when you went through much worse'.

I was dumbfounded, and mortified. Whilst I have never been divorced, I am sure it would in many ways be every bit as traumatic as bereavement to some people.

Will, who had organised the visit to us in hospital, had literally spent the last four days driving around, collecting family from airports and organising hotels and transport, was dead on his feet. His support for us at that time was lifesaving. He had been there on the night and knew nothing about Eamon's prospects until he saw us. The papers in the UK had already reported the death of both of the children, so at least we could provide some hope.

Over the coming days various members of the family were allowed similar limited visits. To be accurate the visitors came to the anteroom and we visited them. Other than my parents and Lucy's who were allowed one visit, only a few others were allowed to see Eamon. The exact details escape me now but I am sure Will saw him. Visits even for us to see him were limited to five minutes each - per day, separately. We were allowed to speak to him and to hold his tiny bandaged hand. It was excruciating but it was gold. Remember; for moments on the night, we were convinced he was dead, even 5% chance of living seemed to us to be a good deal. I know our optimism confounded the staff but they were not where we were… all we had was hope!

Every moment as we lay in our hospital beds, we divined optimism and similarly despair in anything and everything that happened, no matter how small or unconnected to Eamon. We knew Eamon's fight was constant, that any minute of any hour he could give up and be gone. Each time a nurse or doctor entered the room the expectation was bad. The lack of anyone entering the room was good. We would determine that as he had lived past the second day and then the third and then the fourth that this would mean he had a chance, only to be told that the dangerous periods were yet to come, particularly in terms of infection.

The only truly uplifting moment in those early days was on the third or fourth day. The nurses had originally stated that although we could talk to Eamon, he would not hear us due to the depth of his coma. In spite of this a nurse came into our room one day, and asked Lucy to come with her to Eamon's bed side. Naturally, and until we were quickly assured otherwise, we assumed he had died. In fact, Eamon had not evacuated his bowels since being admitted and it was causing problems. The nursing staff hoped that if Lucy could speak to him, or perhaps hold his hand, there might be some reaction. This seemed to contradict what they had previously relayed, but Lucy and I needed no excuse to see him or touch him. It was only the second time we had been allowed into his room together.

Upon entering the cubicle, she leaned over our little son and gently held his hand, she whispered into his ear, her silent tears dropping onto his bandaged head. She kissed him and reassured him it was alright and, in that moment, he emptied his bowels.

Many people in such circumstances have similar accounts of communication where communication is deemed impossible. We never formed any opinion on the matter other than Eamon was inside those bandages and fighting for his life, and he knew we were with him. It was the first and only moment of hope for almost three months, but it was a feast to a starving beast. It fortified us and gave us hope, where previously there had been no hope.

The nursing staff were noticeably friendlier since the police had visited. We assumed that this was because we were by then exonerated from any carelessness or culpability, but we never did discover for sure.

In spite of the better relations with the staff our continuing confinement in the ICU was driving us insane. We requested that we be discharged, and amid much arguments and warnings we were, on about the tenth day, allowed to move into a hotel and be treated as outpatients. A few days later Kirsty's body was, thanks to the tireless efforts of Will, about to be repatriated.

We visited Eamon for five minutes each day and his condition remained unchanged. We started to realise that perhaps the best thing for us and for Eamon, was to return home to bury Kirsty, and then come back to Bordeaux where we could concentrate one hundred percent on him and his recovery, his survival. It was a desperately difficult decision to make but one that we needed to consider.

Lucy asked the surgeon that if we did go back to the UK for three days could they call us if Eamon deteriorated, so we might rush back. The surgeon looked at her as if it was a silly question, and explained that Eamon could not deteriorate further, and that in the time it took the lift to travel from the ICU on the sixth floor to the ground floor, was the time Eamon would have if he got any worse.

It was just another stark exposition of the facts as to how sick Eamon was, but not one that was unexpected, and it did help us to decide to travel back to the UK to bury Kirsty. If Eamon could die while we went for a cup of tea, or to the hotel, or to the toilet, then what difference would distance make? That we would not be able to see him for three days was of minor importance compared with the benefit we would derive from burying Kirsty and returning to concentrate solely on him.

Father's Day

With the decision made we purchased a tape recorder and spent several hours recording nursery rhymes and stories on it. The nursing staff promised to put it on Eamon's pillow and play it every day. We also bought a bottle of Chanel No5, which was the only perfume Lucy ever wore and we scented a couple of soft cloths which we were allowed to leave near his bed. The nurses seemed bemused with the amount of thought we had put into leaving him behind. Racked with guilt, still heavily bandaged we left the hospital and returned to the UK to bury our little girl.

Ireland had just been beaten by Italy one nil in the incredible World Cup of 1990 and Pavarotti was belting out Nessun Dorma from every café and shop in Bordeaux; every one that is which was not playing *Nothing Compares 2u* by Sinead O'Conner.

Chapter Seven

Best Man Dead
(1973)

As children, it was a blessing for my siblings and me that our father's work took him away to foreign countries quite often. The breaks for us from his ruthless and unrelenting discipline, regularly coincided, probably not by coincidence, with the worst of our transgressions.

In addition, as my five brothers and I got older, we became increasingly adept at hiding our misdemeanours, and more and more certain that our mother's protests and assurances that she would tell our father upon his return, from wherever he had gone, were in fact empty threats. She no more wanted him on the rampage than did we, regardless of the reason.

One such transgression occurred shortly after I started secondary school. I had become friendlier with Simon Holden from the hotel in the centre of Bunker's Hill Estate. We'd actually known each other prior to this, but as Simon had gone to the Church of England primary, and I attended Saint Francis, we had initially not really hung out together, until we found ourselves in the Milford Haven Secondary School.

I was, as mentioned, initially assigned to the 'D' Stream. This was the place a child went if they were 'challenged', not as bad as the 'Z' stream, which actually was called the 'Z' stream, and where the kids were given clay or a stick or something and left to it. In the 'D' stream there was a structure and some attempt to teach, if not to learn. The 'Z' stream was more about containment.

Simon and I quickly became inseparable, we would light fires, sneak into the lido, make spears out of bracken, Dutch arrows out of branches, have stone fights with the Swayles family, and do what most kids of our age would do, pretty much anything we were not supposed to do.

Our favourite place to play was the woods. It was everybody's favourite place to play, in spite of it, in our world, being infested with German storm troopers, aliens and many dangerous beasts, including the Blackbridge boys.

Most of the games my brothers, friends and I played were one way or another linked to World War Two. I was born only 16 years after it ended and inevitably, films at that time… the ones I saw on TV and in the cinema, starred the likes of Audie Murphy, John Wayne etc. and were about the war or were westerns. Many adults I knew had fought in the war and it was still, not surprisingly, a very big deal.

My favourite game was 'Best Man Dead'. All the local kids used to play it in the woods at the 'Tump'. The Tump was a small hillock in the centre of the woods. It was probably manmade but I can't say for sure. The game started with one person being nominated as the general, a process often involving huge arguments and sometimes a fight. The general would take position at the very top of the Tump. All the others would take up various positions around its base; they were the enemy soldiers. The general would call out the name of one of the soldiers at random, and the nominated soldier would immediately start running toward him, up the hill. As the soldier hit the base of the Tump the general would defend himself by calling out the name of a weapon, whilst simultaneously firing it, or lobbing it at the assailant. The soldier would respond by dying as spectacularly as he could, as though killed by the weapon nominated.

If the general called out 'rifle' then the soldier would for example usually be hit in the stomach, and grab the wound as they rolled back down the hill. Sometimes a shoulder wound would demand another shot from the general, or if he was inclined, a change of weapon. Nobody ever agreed the rules, it just seemed sensible that if a bullet did not stop the soldier, then it was reasonable to follow up with a hand grenade, or a Samurai sword.

Everyone of course wanted to have 'hand grenade' or 'land mine' called as this provided for the most dramatic death. The general would always remove the safety pin of a grenade with his teeth, and spit it out to the ground before lobbing the explosive at the soldier. It was the only way to arm a hand grenade as any veteran of Best Man Dead or World War Two will tell you.

As each soldier was called and died in their own particular way, they would stay strewn across the ground, where they fell. Many of the soldiers would hide limbs under their bodies to simulate missing arms or legs, some holding imaginary Japanese swords in their bellies, and one or two hiding their heads in their pullovers to signify decapitation. By the end of the game the Tump was littered with kids in various states of contortion. It was for the general then to pick the soldier who had been 'The Best Man Dead', which included not only how they died but also how they presented as a corpse; that person then became the new general and the whole game would start afresh.

It was an enormously popular game of which we never tired. It sometimes attracted twenty or more of us, often from Blackbridge and Bunker's Hill. Sometimes it would go on for hours, with some kids breaking off to go home to have their tea, only to return to re-join, newly invigorated with a full belly and new ways to die.

Originally, we would access the woods over the old sewer pipe but since Judy Coal had fallen in the marsh the whole area had been cordoned off and men were down there digging with machines and repairing the pipe. In the meantime, the only way to the woods was over the new building sites at the bottom of the estate and we had been chased off there several times by the builders, partly I suppose because en-route through the buildings we would be distracted by sand mounds, and nails, and half dry walls we could easily push over.

If we had simply passed through the site there probably would have been less chasings, but less fun too. With the woods effectively temporarily out of bounds we were left to find some other venue of mischief. It was a task to which we all applied ourselves with the utmost vigour, and of course success.

Given Simon's residence in the hotel, opportunities which other kids did not get came our way. Simon discovered that if he left the latch off the toilet window in the cellar bar, he could later, with my help, be lowered down into the toilets and gain easy access to the bar itself.

Once inside Simon would steal all sorts of goodies. Initially for some reason these goodies were confined to drinks mixers like ginger ale, lemonade, bitter lemon and so on. This may seem small chips but to me, an almost 12-year-old boy who did not see lemonade from one month to the next; it was heaven. As with all criminals however we craved bigger and better prizes and soon we were managing to get chocolate bars, cockles, pickled eggs and crisps along with the mixers.

The hotel had several large outbuildings, they even had a horse in a small stable, which never seemed to go anywhere or do anything. Immediately opposite the window into the cellar bar was the barn. On its upper level, hay bales were neatly stacked along with some junk which was stored there. The loft was accessed via a ladder and it was up this ladder and into the back of the barn where we would retreat to scoff and quaff our ill-gotten gains; hiding what we could not devour.

For some reason Simon and I never even considered stealing alcohol in spite of it being the most obvious and easiest thing to steal. That all

Father's Day

changed when Brandon was one day invited to partake of the crisps and other vitals. At our age a 15 or 16-year-old was something to be revered. It was a great honour that he even wanted to spend time with us, so when he proposed Simon be lowered into the bar with a view to retrieving bottles of beer and cigarettes, my friend was only too keen to oblige.

Pretty quickly Brandon was the 'go to' person for alcohol and cigarettes in Milford Haven Secondary School. In fact, he was selling so many cigarettes that Peggy, who owned a little kiosk next to the upper school, and who sold a single cigarette and a match for two pence, was rumoured to be 'after' him for damaging her trade.

Within a few days and in spite of Brandon's supply demands Simon and I had established a stock of cigarettes, beer, spirits, mixers, crisps, chocolate bars, pickled cockles and for some reason, mountains of beer mats. These goodies were all stored in neat piles at the back of the barn, concealed behind two or three hay bales.

The fateful day when the whole caper came to a sudden conclusion was on my twelfth birthday. It was a Monday, and after arriving home from school, I quickly changed out of my uniform and into playing clothes. I gathered up my brothers Will and Edward and we made our way over to the barn. When we arrived Simon was already there, around him about twenty empty cigarette packets. He had opened the packets and laid out in neat rows about four hundred cigarettes. It seemed to me at the time to be a perfectly logical thing to do with cigarettes, and the rows did look very neat. All four of us lit up and started unpacking cigarettes, and forming them into more neat rows. If we had intended to smoke our way through the neat lines we did not get very far.

Neither Simon nor I were smokers, Will and Edward seemed old hands at it however. Pretty soon I felt sick and dizzy… I threw up into the hay and decided enough was enough and made my way into the fresh air and towards home. Shortly after Will followed and finally Edward; all smoked out.

It was just after six pm when we heard the fire engine. I came to the front of the garden and could see the flames licking up behind the hotel across the road. I wondered if it had anything to do with us smoking in the hay filled barn, which definitely was not on fire when I had left it. I concluded it was probably something else.

In the days that followed, incredibly, it turned out that someone unknown had probably left a lit cigarette in one of the barns. There apparently was no evidence of anything else and the culprit was never discovered, but presumed to be Simon. I knew not to look a gift horse in the mouth, so for the purpose of avoiding blame the explanation was fine by me, if everyone else was buying it. Will and Edward certainly agreed it was the most likely explanation.

From that day onwards Simon was forbidden to play with our family, and our father was given a life time ban from the hotel; thus, he had to drink thereafter in the Horse and Jockey.

Although I had a few scrapes before and after the Bunker's Hill Hotel incident I was not generally a naughty child. I thought I was though, thanks in no small part to Brandon who had, amongst other things, convinced me that I was going to be hanged for not returning *Great Expectations* to the library.

Chapter Eight

Hope
(June to September 1990)

So, we return to late spring 1990, some two weeks or so after the accident.

Kirsty's funeral took place in late June in the tiny village of Llangattock, near Crickhowell in South Wales, where Lucy had grown up. We deliberately chose a non-denominational cemetery but allowed my uncle Martin, a priest, along with a pastor from Lucy's parents' church to officiate. Thus, they together would offend everyone or placate everyone. It's odd what religious zealots demand, even of the bereaved.

There can be few things sadder than a three-foot coffin, a tiny hole in the ground and parents burying all their hopes and dreams. We had determined not to cry, or show overt emotion at the funeral, lest it cause others to be overcome, as surely it would.

Our minds were elsewhere, and there was not a moment we were back in the UK that we did not regret the decision to leave Eamon in Bordeaux, but we knew it was the right choice, made in the best interests of our son, who was what mattered now; before Kirsty, before family and before any pointless trip down the road of self-pity.

There would be time for grieving, but it was an indulgence we could not afford at that moment, and not an emotion to be confused with the horror

Father's Day

and bottomless despair of the situation which we endured every day.

The funeral was massively attended with long not seen family from both sides, work colleagues and friends, and even strangers attending. A few from the nuclear station had come and many sent cards of condolence. I felt guilty that I had misjudged some of them as being automatons, many, like us, had children and were clearly affected by our loss. The police blocked off the main street and a TV crew which turned up was asked to keep a respectful distance, which they did.

The service was hard and the interment even harder but we managed to get through it, supporting each other as best we could. We always had something no one else had; each other.

Family and friends who go to funerals, and offer what seem hopeless and inadequate words of support and sympathy, are wrong if they feel the gestures are of little help or comfort. It does help, it helps a huge amount, and it helped us get through the day, and the days to come. Do the awkward thing and don't worry if you get it wrong, that you care enough to try to help is what matters.

Later the Bridge Inn in Crickhowell was given over entirely to our entourage where polite and awkward 'hellos' and sympathies were exchanged. The mood was remarkably positive, and in spite of the situation being tragic, it was of considerable comfort to us, to see so many people re-acquainting themselves in the real and deeply held consideration and love they shared. That in some cases it was transient is not important, at the time and in the moment, it was meant, and it was sincere, and it meant the world to us both.

Early the following morning we were on a plane back to Bordeaux. Just the two of us alone again seemed strange after such a busy few days. People still pushed in in the queue to board the plane, stared at our dressings, raced for the closest overhead locker and so on. Their lives went on uninterrupted and I wanted to stop and shout;

'Don't you know what has happened? Our world is breaking apart and you pushed in in front of us! Is the best locker so important?'

Stopping the world was not an option though, and it was we who must adjust to the situation, not others. I think Lucy tried more than I did, I wanted to be angry and I was angry, at everything and everyone. Even then in those early days I was not the same man I had been a month before. The accident took one child, and at the time maybe them both, but it also took us both, who we were and who we were meant to be. I did not comprehend that at the time of course, nor did Lucy, but years later we both inevitably were drawn to that conclusion. Like a sapling, the damage was planted inside us both but was yet to bear its bitter fruit.

While we were in the UK we tried a few times to phone the hospital, but were unable to get through to the ward. A family friend fluent in French managed to speak to someone who was

Father's Day

reluctant to discuss things with non-family but reported

'No change' on the day of the funeral.

Neither of us could forget the words of the doctor before we left and how change could occur in a matter of seconds at any moment; what was the point of telephoning? It's hard to imagine now in the days of mobile phones and internet but we were pretty much incommunicado as we travelled, cut off from Eamon and those keeping him alive.

Upon landing we got into a taxi and made our way directly to the hospital. Taxi fares were expenditure we could ill afford, and we had already got used to the tram system before leaving, but we needed to get to the hospital as quickly as we could.

Prior to leaving for the UK, we had fallen into a routine determined by the hospital rules. We should only have been allowed one visit per day, for five minutes, for only one person. The hospital relented a little and allowed us both a five-minute visit, provided it was not together.

The routine, which we were to practice every day for almost three months entailed us of arriving in the lobby of the hospital, one of us taking the elevator to the sixth floor, visiting and returning, while the other waited in the lobby, eyes fixed on the elevator doors. The roles would then be reversed while the other visited.

Being the second to visit was always the most excruciating, particularly the first time that our visit coincided with one of Eamon's dressing changes which were carried out under general anaesthetic, so time consuming. Normally the 'sitter' would watch the 'visitor' enter the lift and then wait for the visitor to re-appear in the lobby after their visit. The sitter would then become the visitor.

The first time this coincided with a change of dressings, Lucy was turned away at the ward outer door, I was waiting in the lobby. She knew as she descended in the lift, that upon sight of her coming down so soon, I would inevitably conclude that Eamon had died. With this in mind and in an effort to avoid the unnecessary pain, she started to wave frantically at me even as the doors of the lift opened. Upon seeing the frantic waving from Lucy's still bandaged arms I had of course immediately jumped to the wrong conclusion. It was not until we were upon each other that she said;

'He's alright, just changing dressings; we can go up in an hour'.

We arranged from that day that if for any reason a visit was not possible that the visitor would signal to the sitter all is well, with a simple thumbs-up, and not an impersonation of a bandaged Terpsichore.

On that first day back in France, Lucy came down with her smile, which I could see across the lobby. It was at that moment that we stopped feeling guilty about the decision we had made. Knowing it was probably right would not have helped if Eamon had died in those three days, but in the moment, we no longer needed to consider that. It was the right decision for then, and for the situation, but much later when we eventually had the time to grieve for our daughter, the guilt returned.

I suppose that no decision would have been right, we had done the best we could. We are intelligent people and capable of rationalising even difficult feelings. So why still the guilt? Why the unrelenting ever-present guilt?

'We are alive when she is not'?

'Why is he suffering pain, when we are not'?

In that first visit after the funeral, we noticed that the tape recorder, wrapped in a polythene bag, had been on when we entered Eamon's room. A soft toy, a colourful teddy about six inches tall named Sleeping Pill, which we had bought for him and was previously banned from the ward was also clipped to 'the machine that goes beep' and which kept him alive.

It was the summer of 1990 and temperatures in Bordeaux were record breaking, regularly in excess of 36 degrees. We lived between visits and existed only to see Eamon each day. My weight dropped from an ample fourteen stone to just over 10 and I looked like a vagrant with my skinny legs hanging out of my shorts like twigs.

Lucy too reduced to skin and bone. Neither of us had any appetite and both of us lamented the loss of our interest in food, which previously had been a passion of ours, cooking, eating and sharing.

Several family members visited us during the worst times, most notably my brother Will who was an invaluable support to us both, at great personal cost to himself. My mother and sister Leonora visited briefly also, which was a pleasant but unexpected surprise. It can't have been easy for them given the circumstances.

Various members of Lucy's family also visited, but in spite of their good intentions, we really just wanted to be alone. They did nothing to help the situation and the distraction I assume they had intended to be was one that was not welcome.

I don't blame them, we just had things on our minds and behaving conventionally was not one of them. We found the expectation to be 'normal' was unexpected. Explaining ourselves was not something we'd anticipated. We were not just grieving for Kirsty; we were terrified that the next moment would bring us more tragedy, something we both knew was a real possibility, almost a certainty, but others did not seem to grasp. We also were recovering from our own physical injuries and doing our best in unchartered waters… as, to be fair, I suppose were they to some extent, but we did not feel the need to dissect their every move or utterance.

One decidedly unpleasant visitor was my Uncle Martin or 'Father Benedict' as he was better known in his parish back in the UK. I'd pretty much never seen this particular uncle, but he had shared officiation at Kirsty's funeral; he was after all a priest and in the family. I disliked priests intensely, I still do, all of them, without exception.

It seemed odd to both Lucy and me at the time that he came and stayed in Bordeaux with us for almost two weeks. He was an utterly loathsome creature. In common with most Catholic priests which I have met, he was spectacularly selfish. He got drunk regularly, and on one particular night was screaming obscenities to the point that he was asked to leave the hotel; only to resolve the issue the next morning by donning his collar and receiving the appropriate consideration for a man of his station. We moved hotel the next day which although further from the hospital, was also further from him.

Our curiosity and surprise as to why he was in France was later answered when a woman with whom he had a relationship appeared in the centre pages of the Sunday Mirror. The article was published on August 1990 but we did not see it until after we returned to the UK over a month later. In short, everyone knew but us.

The woman 'spilt the beans' about him and their affair and their child, whom she claimed he had abandoned. In a letter which he actually wrote from our hotel in Bordeaux he claimed to 'walk with God', as one does… he claimed to have not run away but instead to be supporting us as we had lost our 'son' in a fire.

Either he had a premonition, an inaccurate one, or he really did not know it was our daughter who had died. I believe Panorama did a piece on him also. We had thought it odd he was in France and he certainly was no support, he was a drain on our resources and our emotions.

As it happened, I have never had an issue with priests having sex, provided it is not with 10-year-old school boys, which it too often seems to be; though thankfully not in his case. What I had an issue with was the gluttony, the selfishness and the lies, hiding from his shame, while pretending to help us. Our experience with him did nothing for my growing misanthropy; or is that everything for it?

For most of the time in France we were alone. We spent days in the park in the scorching heat playing backgammon or under the Monument aux Girondins on the riverfront with our feet in the water of the fountain under the huge bronze horses, waiting for the next hospital visit, dreading the next hospital visit.

The Tall Ships came and went, and the weeks passed. Time dragged like a lead cloak on a weary traveller but every day one more step to hope, one more day not dead, one more day alive.

Each morning, we would ride the tram from the hotel room in the centre of the city, up to the hospital on the outskirts to visit our son. Each morning the same terrible wait for one or the other to give the 'thumbs up'; the utterly awful 'jambon sandwich' and excellent coffee from the hospital café. How do the French eat sandwiches without butter? Each day the doctors confirming the same pessimistic prognosis like some torturous contortion of Groundhog Day.

By the second month Eamon had contracted, and battled past, one infection after another only then to have acquired a methicillin-resistant staphylococcus, or the 'Super Bug' as tabloids named it some years after, when it became the 'must-have' infection for any clinically on point hypochondriac.

Heavy duty intravenous antibiotics followed into the second month, with heavier duty antibiotics after that, in what seemed to be an everlasting torment for our child and for us.

Time lost meaning, days and nights did not matter; only the visits mattered. With distance and areas, one could use patronising and annoying tabloid reference points such as 'London buses' or 'football pitches' or even the area of Wales when it concerned the rain forest, but what was there for our situation? Three months to Christmas perhaps? Three months jail time, three months to childbirth… tangible, manageable and with an end in sight but this three months was endless.

Three months of every morning on a tram ride with a notion of the last stop, but no idea of the real destination. Each day we would travel to Eamon's bedside knowing that he might have breathed his last minutes before our visit… or would do seconds after.

I knew what a five percent chance meant, it meant;

'No chance but we can't say that'.

We learned some time later that the team in the hospital had considered ending life support, because the prospects for Eamon were all but hopeless. This might seem a hard decision, and of course it is, but if someone less badly injured could be saved with the limited resource, the situation might be two dead and not one. Eamon took up an ultra-high ICU bed, and many life support resources for three months, it could not go on for ever and we knew that.

A few years later Lucy helped Eamon's surgeon, the wonderful Mr Andrew Burd, deliver a lecture to trainee doctors on the matter of ethics, and specifically at what stage seriously burned patients should be allowed to expire without intervention. How can it even be a question?

Day in and day out, our little boy fought on, his fifth birthday came and went, he did not have a party, but he lived another day, and another day after, and another again after that, until miracle of miracles, that thing we never even dared speak to each other, or even think possible… happened.

It really happened, and it happened to us, and even now I find it hard to believe. It was the beginning, and we could not believe it, and all we could feel was happiness and confusion and sadness and anger and regret but most of all … hope!

It was a morning in mid-September, already close to thirty degrees and humid. The air conditioning in the hospital was welcome relief as we entered.

Lucy had gone to the sixth floor in accord with our by now familiar routine, but she came back down again within a few minutes. I saw her immediately; no thumb, my heart hit the floor, she was waving and running towards me, no bandages just the scars on her arms now, a long time had passed. The delight in her face dawned on me and from the depths I resurfaced, like that first gasp of air three months before, I could breathe again and I knew it would be fresh clean air and not the heat of despair and destruction I inhaled.

I dropped my sandwich and rushed towards her, arms outstretched, we embraced, I held her and she held me; she was barely able to speak through sobs which emanated from her very core and reverberated into my own body and into my soul.

'He's awake, he's awake, he's awake.' Her body racked against mine with her sobs of relief and joy; she could not stop saying it, as though had she done, it would escape and we would rewind groundhog style.

Still afraid to let go of the awful void that had replaced hope for so long, I dragged her into the lift and within minutes we were entering the ICU outer unit, and then into the inner. Two nurses, whom Lucy and I by now knew well, at the sight of us simultaneously burst into tears and excitedly guided us into our Eamon's glass cage.

Incredibly, there he was, still completely bandaged from head to knees and with loose dressings on his feet, his shins the only part not covered in some form of dressing. He was propped up on pillows with his eyes wide open and blinking. We could actually see his long eyelashes which for some reason had escaped the flames. Tubes still stretched out from his torso and both arms but one less in his mouth. The football was still and silent.

He was breathing unaided, rasping and strained but unaided. Lucy approached him, hesitated and looked to one of the nurses for approval. The nurse smiled a smile concealed by her surgical mask, but which her eyes telegraphed. She leaned over and kissed our son on the side of his head, and it turned, almost imperceptibly, towards her, it was as though his eyes, both shining with tears, had forced his head to move as he looked to her;

'Happy Birthday' she said. She reassured him, and stroked him and her gentle words fell on him and his tears abated.

I reached for Sleeping Pill and gently walked him up Eamon's leg to his chest. His eyes followed it, and then turned to mine and they smiled at me. It was almost completely overwhelming, but I kept my composure, as though Eamon had just fallen off his bike, and there was nothing to worry about.

The doctors were swift to warn of elevated expectations, explaining that Eamon had serious infections still and remained on renal support, but it was impossible to subdue the utter elation and inevitable optimism we both felt. The staff could hardly conceal their own delight and pride in having held onto his life against all odds and expectations and for so long.

The five minutes turned into twenty-five minutes and finally, as we left, kissing and hugging the nurses, all of whom by now were in floods of tears, we could barely believe what had just happened. Could it really be over?

Scrambling in pockets and wallets for phone cards, we took up position at phone boxes at each end of the lobby, and exploded the news to every family member and friend we could manage, before our cards ran out… then we bought more cards from the little cubicle opposite the lifts and made more calls.

As we stepped out of the hospital hand in hand the weather broke, a sudden heavy downpour dragging the heat from the day. As the clouds cleared, a new freshness descended on the city and we could breathe.

Whilst almost overcome with optimism and relief we both knew there was a long road to go, but the odds now looked distinctly in Eamon's favour. His progress over the following couple of weeks was astonishing. He had teetered on the brink for months and now was back. Within a week he was off renal support and undergoing gentle physiotherapy. The prognosis included him losing most of his fingers and perhaps a hand, but he eventually defied even that when he lost just part of one finger.

By the third week the bandages had been removed from his head, and were replaced by loose dressings, dressings he would have on his head for over a year as the wounds slowly closed. His face and scalp were terribly burned, and over the months the surgeons harvested and re-harvested the skin from his thighs, calves and shins, which were pretty much the only unburned parts of his body. Several grafts had taken well on his face. His torso had been totally 'de gloved' as had most of his arms and remained mostly skinless. What little skin they could harvest, had to be stretched and placed in the worst areas, and would thus grow together and form multiple keloid scars. He was going to need to undergo many months of grafting, and then years of re-grafting and contracture release surgery but he was going to live. We were warned of the potential of brain damage and possible amputations but he was going to live… he was going to live.

Eamon was getting stronger by the day, by the hour. Every day stronger made him less vulnerable, made us more optimistic. He was still unable to speak and would be for several months more, his Ryle's tube was still in place for feeding but he could and often did smile around it. He could almost hug us and was able to communicate with nods, smiles, frowns and shakes of the head. Incredibly he was happy, as he always had been before the accident. His stoicism was a quality he took from his mother and it never failed to impress me.

Eamon accepted his predicament with heroic indifference, as we tried our best to explain what had happened in terms he could understand. The task of telling him his sister was gone was one we avoided at that time, assuring him she was in another place and very happy.

Father's Day

By the end of September, he was eating naturally, baby food mostly and ice-cream. And we took it in turns to feed him. We contemplated all the parents in the world who complained about such a task, and pitied them for missing the sublime pleasure they could derive from it.

He was eventually allowed visitors other than us and we were given permission to arrange an air ambulance to fly him to a hospital in the UK.

A couple of weeks later he was rolled out of the ward and into the lift in a fully tented surgical bed. The doctors and nurses, several in tears wished us luck with handshakes and hugs and kisses on cheeks, with more than French civility - with affection. We could barely see our way for the tears of joy, hope, desperation and exhaustion.

In moments we were in the waiting blue cross ambulances heading for the airport; Eamon and me in one and Lucy in another. At the airport we were waved straight to a waiting air ambulance and along with two nurses and a doctor we took to the air, homeward bound. We were going back to the UK, but never really back home. It was the second-best day of our lives so far, the first had been only weeks before.

Chapter Nine

Eamon
Long and Winding Road to Recovery
(1990)

Eamon was discharged from the hospital in Chepstow in late December 1990 and after numerous surgeries was released from the ICU directly to his mother's care. In spite of relations between the nurses and us sometimes being difficult the surgical staff could see Lucy was by far more competent a carer than anyone else. This was due to a combination of her natural love for her son but also to her very measured and intelligent approach. She was after all a little more invested in Eamon's whole wellbeing than anyone else might be.

We managed to buy a house in the town so as to be near to Will and Karen and the children, whose support was absolutely invaluable in those early days. Initially, as the purchase went through, we stayed with them, and it was a bit of a crush. My company offered to pay for a hotel, but that would have been unsuitable for Eamon so we declined.

Will and Karen gave us their room and the kids were exceptionally gentle and kind to their cousin, who was of course still exceptionally poorly. Thankfully the house purchase was concluded within about six weeks and we moved into our own place, not 200m from them.

Eamon's confinement, including in France had been for some six months or so and while in the 10-bed unit in Chepstow, he was out of danger, so underwent mostly grafting operations. By the time he was allowed home much of his body had been grafted but there were still many areas of exposed flesh, some of which took hours to dress daily. His scalp remained mostly an open wound, which gradually was closing.

For some reason, before arriving in the hospital in the UK Eamon had not been screened for MRSA and upon his arrival in the ten-bed ICU burns unit, he was discovered to have a very virulent one, as I have mentioned. It was not a danger to him as he'd acquired it gradually and built an immunity in France, but it could have been fatal to other patients.

The unit was emptied but for him. All of the equipment from beds to monitors had to be sent to Swansea for decontamination. He was the only burns victim allowed in the unit for some time. We were not popular with the hospital and some of the staff made that very plain indeed, in spite of it being their error.

As part of his treatment at home and unquestionably the most traumatic for him and for Lucy was the requirement to regularly scrub the scabs off his healing scalp. This was necessary to allow the wound to heal in a particular way. He would be placed in the bath and she had to literally scrape the dead skin off, as the healing progressed gradually.

It was beyond excruciating for Eamon, who had never before or after ever complained of pain. Many evenings his screams could be heard from outside our house on Delkin Road in Dursley. Lucy and Eamon would both be in tears, and she tried everything she could to reduce the pain, but it just had to be done. She would afterwards lie on his bed cuddled up to his back, sobbing as she stroked his skin as he fell to sleep. It was in fact almost a full year after the accident before his scalp closed up completely and the MRSA was finally gone.

Eamon did not return to school full time until he was almost seven. In that time Lucy taught him at home so although he kept up with his schoolwork when he did return, he had a good deal of catching up to do socially. He was however, by then, a good reader and as good at most lessons as his classmates.

A wonderful woman named Mrs Philpot used to come to the house twice a week to teach him also, and give Lucy the respite she neither asked for nor wanted, but welcomed. He was for the most part still wheelchair bound and when he went back to school, he spent many periods in various slings and splints as each of the operations to release skin contractures progressed.

The releasing or 'z plasty' operations were a constant in his childhood, and into his adolescence. Indeed, he occasionally still has these operations, well into his thirties. No sooner had he recovered from one operation he was on the operating table for another.

He wore compression suits over his body, his face arms and hands most of his childhood, in an effort to reduce keloid scarring, and these were intensely uncomfortable and hot and made him itch. Little patches of blood were regularly left on door frames and along the woodchip paper in the hall and landing, where he would rub himself until he bled through the pressure garments. He had also lost almost all of his sweat glands as a result of the burns and this served to make the garments even more uncomfortable.

By the time he was home, we noticed his hearing was getting very poor and as though he needed any more challenges, and we needed any more bad news, it was discovered that he was going deaf. At first, we had no idea why or how bad it would get. The deafness it turned out was the result of the powerful antibiotics he had been given in France to combat the many infections. We were told it would plateau, hopefully before total deafness but there was no way to say for sure. As the months passed his hearing dropped severely and was total in several ranges but did eventually plateau, at a severe loss and not total.

He was fitted with bi-lateral hearing aids and that helped a great deal but they were cumbersome and uncomfortable and because he was limited in where he could sweat from, they kept breaking down due to being wet.

When his hearing loss seemed to plateau, we were not thankful for small mercies, we were angry for so few. With hearing aids, it was manageable, though difficult for him, particularly in school where they made what accommodation their resources allowed. His head teacher, the fantastic Mrs Jones did what her budget allowed and was a huge support to him and to us.

A huge part of his recovery socially and emotionally was due to his wonderful cousins, Marie, Kate and Jake; they had been present at the scene of the accident. In fact, as mentioned, when he was first allowed 'home' it was to their home with us that he returned while we sorted out a place for ourselves.

The children played with and helped him assimilate and were fiercely protective of him, often unnecessarily so. Marie and Kate were particularly close to him and there is no question that he would not have made the early progress to recovery he did without them onside.

It was a squeeze in my brother's house but very soon we were settled in the area in which we needed to be, and we devoted ourselves to doing the best we could for our son.

Along with the house move came a transfer of employment for me, from where over the following few years I progressed from CAD operator in the drawing office into project management, in civils and then into the emerging world of fibre optics in telecommunications.

As time passed Eamon's operations became part of the routine of his life, and of ours and he progressed well, physically, mentally and socially. Lucy had given up her job as a manager in a

Father's Day

supermarket chain after the accident and dedicated herself to his care. As a result, Eamon would regularly have major operations and be released into her care within days whereas normally such procedures would require many weeks of hospital confinement. There was little she did not know about the aftercare required, and was held in the highest regard by all of the medical professionals who encountered her.

Eamon as a child, was also, in spite of his injuries, a very cheerful and active little chap. He never allowed his disability, nor indeed his particular state of mobility at any particular time between operations, to stop him from playing with his cousins or the other children in the area. He would from time to time be confined to a wheel chair, or be splinted in various odd contortions required to ensure the correct healing process, and minimise contractures, but nothing stopped him playing.

On one occasion his right arm was splinted at right angles to his body and in plaster. His entire torso was in a cast, and as an added impediment to enjoyment outdoors his neck was in a brace, lifting his chin so he could, unlike the proverbial dog in urban myth, only look up, or was it not look up? Add to this the pressure garments, dressing changes etc. and no one could have blamed him for being miserable, but he literally never was.

He was contorted as described for almost eight weeks. By the end of this time, he had become adept at rushing around and leaning to the left, raising his extended limb appropriately whenever he encountered obstacles. He had this skill down to a fine art; often his hand or head passing, at speed, within millimetres of objects, never actually hitting them.

He demonstrated this unusual skill when aged about 11. Being unable to use his skateboard in the conventional way, he had already discovered that he could instead sit on it, and roll down the footpath outside of our house at breakneck speeds, steering with remarkable agility and accuracy, simply by leaning one way or the other. In fact, the method had become so popular with the other children, that hardly anyone in the area for years was seen standing upright on a skateboard.

As much as we tried to dissuade him from sitting on the contraption while he was in the splint with his arm protruding outwards, we ultimately had to give in and he was allowed to ride from the top of the short driveway down its slope to the garage door, always with his helmet on and never to progress outside the drive. This seemed to satisfy him and he, along with his cousins and his best friend Steve, spent his time within the confinement of the drive.

One of the maxims which I learned from my father, was that when children suddenly are very quiet, there is a good chance that they are up to no good. One day, with this in mind and with no noise from the driveway I went outside to check. Eamon was nowhere to be seen and as I approached the top of the drive, his best friend Steven, belly flat on his skateboard, came whizzing past, down the footpath, which ran parallel to the house, with all the speed of a torpedo but none of its control.

I stepped onto the path and turning right looked up its one-hundred-and-twenty-foot length to see a little congregation of children holding their skateboards and 'stacking' in much the same way as planes might, as they wait to land. Eamon, at the front of the queue, evidently the next to depart, was sitting upright on his board, his arm sticking out from his body, as though he were signalling to turn right.

Before I could object Marie gave the board and Eamon a hefty shove, and he rapidly began accelerating down the steeply graded open pathway with nothing between him and me. Nothing that is but a concrete lamp post set into the footpath leaving a gap of less than two foot six inches between it, and the garden wall of our neighbour.

I did not know for sure what Eamon measured from fully extended arm to opposite shoulder, I'd never thought to check, but given that the boy had to turn sideways to get through door openings I guessed it was considerably more than two foot six inches.

Eamon may or may not have seen me; his mind was more than likely consumed with the journey, which even without the obstacle was treacherous enough. It looked certain that as a minimum he was going to hit the concrete lamp post with his elevated limb.

Plaster cast or not he would certainly break it at the speed he was travelling. I almost closed my eyes as he was upon the obstacle, but I am glad that I did not. Without the least hesitation or concern he, with perfect timing and extraordinary accuracy leaned to his left, thus raising his right arm to within millimetres of the post and his head to within a similar perilous distance from the wall.

This explained the scratches on the top of his crash helmet, which recently had appeared. On he went to the bottom of the hill, expertly around the bend to where a natural stop could be achieved.

When he returned on foot a moment or two later it was with a beaming smile and what was obviously enormous pride; his skateboard under his left arm with his right sticking out like a wing indicator on an early Morris Minor. Far from being angry I gushed with amazement and enthusiasm and had him repeat the feat but only after getting Lucy to come witness it.

Over his growing years Eamon time and time again illustrated his remarkable courage and absolute belief in himself. A belief which more often than not was justified but sometimes was not, and in fact occasionally defied logic; for example; some years later when we were renovating his first home in Cardiff, he decided that rather than employ a plasterer he would teach himself how to plaster… from a DVD. The results looked as though someone had applied the plaster with a hand grenade and not a float.

Father's Day

Eamon definitely had his limitations; he just needed to find them himself and not be told them. It's one of the very best things about my son.

Chapter Ten

Eamon
The Swimmer
(1995)

The most notable, or most memorable example of Eamon's character, courage and determination was one neither we nor many others who witnessed it will ever forget. I am going to tell you about it now because, as you will see, it exemplifies the very best of everything about him, indeed about others just like him who overcome the most challenging of things every day. The ordinary things.

So; it was not achieving his Veterinary Degree or his Masters in 2010; it was not getting into Vet School against all the odds; it was not being given an award by Princess Dianna for bravery, nor indeed the Lord Lieutenant's medal for bravery; it was not his Duke of Edinburgh Gold award; it was not carrying the Olympic Torch in 2012; or indeed marrying the most beautiful girl in Liverpool, nor was it owning his own practice, aged just 29, or his second practice at age 33... or the countless other things he has achieved so far. It was at a gala in our local swimming pool when he was not yet 11 years old. Here is why:

He had been in the Cubs until aged about 10 and loved it. He was new to the Scouts and was always an enthusiastic member but very limited in what he could do. Many of the tasks were beyond

Father's Day

him simply because he had extremely limited use of his limbs and anyway, was in and out of hospital so regularly that he missed many of the meetings. Sometimes he would attend in his wheelchair, and just be happy to be sporting his little brown scarf, and those badges he had so far achieved.

His Scout master was exceptionally kind, as were his fellow Scouts and when the time came for the annual swimming gala between local Scout groups, they selected Eamon to be in the four-man relay team. I had taught him, to swim in the local pool, and it was an important part of his physio, so most Saturdays you could find us there, with or without his cousins. Given his limitations he could only really doggy paddle because both armpits and elbows at the time were severely contracted and he could barely lift his arms to forty degrees from his body.

In fact, the operation which left him splinted at ninety degrees shortly after the gala, and mentioned in the previous chapter had begun the process of releasing his skin in that area to improve movement. He could not even get close to breast stroke and of course over arm was out of the question. Eamon could barely reach to scratch his own face without having to bring his head down to meet his hand when he needed to do so, which was frequent due to the pressure garments he wore, including a full facemask.

Another aspect of regular swimming was to get Eamon used to the staring, which he would inevitably encounter his whole life. Lucy and I very consciously spent a great deal of time and effort preparing him for this and we both like to think that we did a very good job of it. I am sure those afternoons swimming in Dursley pool did get him prepared for it to some extent, and more able to deal with it appropriately.

I think his mother's genes too contributed greatly to his exceptional outlook on life, and the ability to live with, what after all, he had to live with. Had he only had my genes he'd have been angry and bitter. That is not self-effacement, it's just a fact. Some people deal with these things heroically and some do not; which would you say are the more content? Acceptance of a predicament when you can't change it is not defeatism, it is realism and it is rare. I number Katie Piper amongst such people and have a huge amount of admiration for her because of it.

Eamon was never going to win any swimming race but by putting him into the relay, the last race of the day, the organisers were giving him the opportunity to take part. Over the years I have heard many people speak against such inclusion and I become incensed at the thinking of those who have issues against it, all of whom seem to be able in body, but not in mind or spirit.

Eamon was selected to go last; each child being required to complete two lengths of the twenty-five-metre pool. It was indoors and all the staff knew the family well, as did the local children and only occasionally would anyone stare at Eamon. We had many conversations with him about his

Father's Day

scars and other issues relating to the accident, and he was comfortable with his predicament even from a very early age.

Unquestionably the community in Dursley, particularly his cousins, had contributed to his absolute acceptance of the situation. That said, he was and remains the most severely scarred person most people would ever encounter. He understood that people would inevitably sometimes stare, and that was OK, it had to be. His reaction was always to smile back. Not sarcastically or pointedly but kindly and warmly.

That day the pool was packed with Scouts and their respective leaders, and assistants at each end of the pool and along one side. On the opposite side was the open viewing area where bench seats gradually elevated away from the poolside. Every seat was taken with proud and enthusiastic parents, many more were standing.

Eamon waited patiently at the entrance end of the pool, with his team, and looked around keenly trying to read lips as his hearing aids were out, lest they get wet. Due maybe in part to this he noticed more than the usual elongated stares from the visitors but seemed not to be too bothered. We stood behind him alongside other parents who could not get a perch in the gallery.

The event went well and the supporters and teams cheered enthusiastically as each event unfolded. Finally came the relay race; four boys stood in line at the end of each of the five lanes. Eamon, not in the least nervous stood at the back of his line and did his best to understand what was being announced over the speaker system, by reading the reactions of the other boys.

When his team was named, he reacted, albeit with a slight delay, with typical yelping and clapping along with his friends, who patted encouragement into each other's shoulders.

The whistle went, and the first line dived into the pool and off they went. The crowd cheered and continued to shout encouragement at the first turn, with one lad starting to break free on account of a turn worthy of Johnny Weissmuller at the first twenty-five metres. As each swimmer reached the end of their second length, they tagged the next and with minimal separation they one by one plopped into the water and resurfaced, all doing the crawl. By the time Eamon stood at the end of the pool ready to be tagged, his team was a good few yards ahead.

He'd been offered by the organisers the opportunity to be in the water ready to kick off, due to being unable to dive in, but had firmly rejected the chance. Thus, when the third boy tagged Eamon's foot he simply turned around and slipped into the pool, kicked off and started to doggie paddle.

Eamon was for a moment in the lead due to the efforts of his three preceding team mates. The cheering continued but we detected a distinct lowering of the noise and enthusiasm. Perhaps it would have been ungracious of the parents and teachers to overly encourage the next boy who was rapidly catching Eamon, and passing him, as within a few strokes did the other teams. As Eamon reached the end of his first length the other boys had already completed their second and thus the race itself, and they were getting out of the pool.

Eamon touched the far side of the pool. His team and several others were cheering, but by now the place was almost silent, confused perhaps in how to react.

Eamon's Scout leader, seeing the comparative snail's pace of his swimming, had already walked to the end of the pool as Eamon got there, ready to turn. The man reached down and touched him on the head with the unmistakeable invitation to call it a day and exit the pool. No one would have been concerned, as Eamon had given his all, he had done his best.

Eamon however made a most obvious refusal; his indignation was palpable… He turned and could see the others standing at the end of the pool and in an almost amused, even contemptuous motion dismissed the leader and launched himself, alone in the water, on his last length.

The entire place erupted. To a single person everyone started cheering at the very tops of their voices. Teachers, children, parents and even the lifeguards many of whom did not even know his name… by now found themselves chanting it. It was impossible to imagine the uproar getting louder, yet it did. As he crossed the halfway line the entire place was on its feet. I could barely see for the tears that filled my eyes. My heart was almost bursting with pride. On and on Eamon crept forwards, occasionally spitting out a mouthful of water, until finally he reached the end of the pool and clearly, even he could hear the uproar.

His team jumped into the water and lifted him aloft, or tried to; the other teams joined them in the water. Mothers and even team leaders were openly weeping at the sight of this extraordinary little boy illustrating in five minutes what his life had to that point and would continue to exemplify: courage, strength of character, an incapacity to feel self-pity and most of all, the single worst swimming skill ever witnessed in Dursley Pool.

No one will recall the team or individual who won gold that day, simply because Eamon was gold and he shone and no one who was there will ever forget it, least of all Lucy and me.

Lucy turned in tears to me and put up her thumb, 'He's awake' she said.

Chapter Eleven

Eamon
Growing Older

Remarkably, for the early years Eamon was never bullied or treated unkindly, though as he entered his teenage years, we had to relocate to Yorkshire for reasons beyond our control, and things changed.

He was relentlessly bullied in one school, Howden Secondary School. We approached the headmaster and he assured us that there was no bullying in his school, so much so in fact that he had no need of an anti-bullying policy, which I asked to see. He had that in common with the Local Education Authority at the time. There was apparently so little bullying that they needed no policy for it. This was not 1964, it was 1998 and the LEA had no anti bullying policy? I even wrote to the Secretary of State for Education but they were just not interested.

There are some battles one cannot win, in particular; teachers, general practitioners, the police, local government officials and so on, so it's often best to find a way around them, rather than to lock horns with them.

We moved Eamon to a private school to get him away from the bullies. The LEA reacted by removing his hearing appliances because we had 'chosen' to school him privately. In spite of East

Gavin O'Donnell

Riding of Yorkshire's best efforts, Eamon thrived in the private school.

University was a revelation for him. He defied all expectations, other than ours, and his own, and got a place in Veterinary School in Liverpool, where he was the first severely hearing-impaired student to study to train as a Veterinary Surgeon. Following his first year, in part due to the success he had made of it, a hearing-impaired young woman was also given a place to study veterinary science.

Lucy and I had never thought that his desire to be a Veterinary Surgeon was anything particularly ambitious. We were not oblivious to the obstacles he would need to overcome but overcoming obstacles was what he did, all his short life. He was a very bright boy, and as soon as he had learned to read, he was almost never seen without a book, preferring them to TV due to his hearing difficulties.

Our hopes for Eamon, and indeed his own expectations were once challenged on an open day at his sixth form school where he was studying Physics, Chemistry and Biology at 'A' Level. Eamon was seventeen and clearly a very competent student, though not always 'A' grade it has to be said, for obvious reasons.

On the day in question his teacher took us out of earshot of Eamon and with his hand considerately placed over his mouth to speak to us, expressed his doubts. The teacher had with the best intention suggested that we were perhaps giving

Eamon 'unrealistic ambitions' by encouraging him to be a Vet. He actually used those words.

The school already had learned quickly and with embarrassment of Eamon's exceptional lip-reading ability and whilst the gesture of the teacher covering his mouth was perhaps necessary, it confirmed to Eamon that the conversation was not for his ears, nor indeed his eyes. Hearing people can only guess when they are being spoken about; the deaf tend to know for sure.

We were undeterred but slightly bewildered by the teacher's unflinching lack of confidence in our son. Eamon had missed huge sections of his education and yet was still regularly top of his class in possibly the three hardest subjects.

When I accompanied him to his interview to Liverpool and Bristol Universities the course leaders had been very keen to point out that without a triple 'A' in their results the students had little hope of entry onto the massively oversubscribed course.

During his two year 'A Level' course Eamon missed over a third of his academic timetable due to a series of very successful contracture operations in Pinderfields hospital and resulting convalescences. We knew he would struggle to get the three 'A' grades, mainly due to this.

I was in work when Eamon's results came through. He'd managed an 'A' in Biology, a 'B' in Physics and a 'B' in Chemistry. They were relatively disappointing results of course but exceptional given the circumstances. I emphasise the word 'relatively'… they were considerably better than anything I ever achieved.

I was at my desk in an open plan office when I heard the news. I promptly telephoned the head of the course in Liverpool and remarkably managed to get her first time, on a day where innumerable other over bearing parents were no doubt making similar calls.

I began to explain why Eamon should be given a place in spite of his results not being quite good enough. The woman stopped me mid-sentence, appearing at first to be frustrated with what was inevitably her tenth or twentieth similar call and said;

'I remember meeting him on the open day and again on the day of his interview and I can confirm we are offering him a place'.

I felt my eyes immediately fill; I assume with sweat… she continued:

'Eamon is the sort of young man we want in our institution'.

I burst into tears, definitely tears and not sweat… much to the surprise and concern of my colleagues sitting nearby.

It is the case that for every bully, incompetent professional or member of the public who had stared at Eamon and even Veterinary Practices who refused to employ what was clearly an exceptional Vet, there were at least three or four exceptional and kind people who from time to time gave Eamon the benefit of the doubt and maybe even an 'unfair' advantage over the next person, but in reply Eamon always dumbfounded expectations.

Over the years he encountered many people, including health professionals, educators and others. He from time to time won small accolades such as medals of courage, as mentioned and these really did mean a lot to him, and to us. It was clear that people admired him for his qualities, but few ever really knew him the way his mother and sister Megan and I know him. The most notable exception was, and is, the student he met at a Halloween fancy dress party in university in Liverpool, and who later became his wife; her name is Fiona.

Fiona is exceptionally attractive; one of those girls whom most men would never approach due to the likelihood of being rejected. She'd seen Eamon around campus once or twice in the huge 4.2 Litre, V8, Vintage Jaguar XJ I had rebuilt and been badgered to lend to him for a term. It was a wreck but much like Eamon, it stood out from the crowd, for all the right reasons. Eamon, although never a big head or boastful was never encumbered with self-doubt either. He was as good as and not better than anyone else, we always assured him of this, and we did not lie.

He'd approached Fiona at the party and offered to buy her a drink; she accepted and then had to find the money to pay for it... and his, as he had no cash left on him. She paid for the drinks for the remainder of the night. They have been inseparable since.

An intelligent and forthright woman who saw the depths to Eamon and was devoted to him for every right reason, and there are many. She is a fiery Irish girl, partial to a Pot Noodle but a devoted wife to Eamon and mother to their son Edward, who arrived on Christmas day in 2015. She is perfect for him and he is for her, though she is unfamiliar with the mysteries of a clothes iron.

Who of us could have foreseen such a wonderful life for that little boy lying unconscious amongst all those machines in a French hospital?

When he qualified as a vet in 2010, he had already achieved an interlocutory Masters in Animal Infectious Diseases which he studied in New Zealand, the dissertation upon which was published. He was awarded a meritorious prize for his work in the university and voted in the yearbook, by his co students, as the graduate most likely to own his own surgery the soonest.

They were right. Upon leaving university as qualified as any of his friends and more than most he attended numerous interviews but was able only to secure work as a locum. By the end of six months, he was the only Liverpool Vet graduate that year, without a full-time position; coincidence perhaps?

Incredibly and in blatant contravention of all disability laws, then and now, his hearing issues were several times cited as a reason for him not being successful. I suggested taking action but Eamon, through bitter experience, and by far the calmer and wiser in the matter of prejudice, knew only too well how small a world the vet world is and the potential of such adverse notoriety to his career.

As usual he soldiered on. Eventually an Irish gentleman who owned a practice in South Wales gave him two days a week as a locum with the promise of it being steady at least for a year or so as he was himself winding down to retirement.

Within two months Eamon was working there full time, within twelve months he and his colleague had bought the practice with the help of yet another of those helpful people he occasionally encountered, this time, remarkably in the form of a bank manager. Two years after that he built and opened a second practice, which was soon thriving? He then became the sole owner of both practices, employing some 27 people, including 7 vets. He was still in his thirties. The yearbook had been correct, so were we, so was Eamon.

He plans in the near future to build and run an animal hospital near Cardiff. I'm not betting against it.

Chapter Twelve

Megan
(1994)

As the years passed, we tried to live as ordinary a life as possible and for the most part we succeeded. Lucy's care for Eamon was nothing less than extraordinary, but we wanted to move on with our lives, we wanted more children.

Within a couple of years of the accident we decided to look into the adoption process. We were accepted onto the 'Catholic Children's Society' training course in Bristol and our appointed trainer was a woman in her sixties. She had never married or had children, natural or adopted, but she was a trained social worker so knew her beans when it came to raising children – one must suppose.

I forget her name but remember that she several times warned us of the dangers of adopting to replace a lost child, and then put us on a course with two other sets of prospective adopters, both of whom had lost children.

She expressed concern when I gently and jokingly enquired if we could change the name of any female child we might adopt to 'Kirsty'; and dye her hair blonde. They say that a sense of humour is the very last step in evolution and she was living proof of it.

After a suitable scolding from Lucy, I kept my head down and did not look the woman in the eye again; we were approved as adopters some time in 1992 or maybe 93, I can't recall exactly.

The reasons we had gone for adoption were twofold. First; even before we got married, we had agreed that it was something we would do regardless of having our own children. There seemed to us to be a certain wastefulness to people having many children of their own and not adopting those without parents. Simplistic I know but true, I think.

Of course, many adopters adopt for reasons other than just the inability to have children of their own and I have always found that very comforting, it is good to know there are such people around. I am an admitted, indeed proud misanthrope, as anyone can tell, but even I recognise that there is some good in some people, and I like it when I encounter it. I suppose the rarer anything is, the more valued it might be.

The second factor influencing our decision was that we could not have any more children naturally. When Kirsty was just a toddler, Lucy became pregnant again but unfortunately, she miscarried midterm.

I mentioned this in a previous chapter. At the time, whilst a traumatic event it was not the end of the world. We'd both been sad at the loss, and Lucy spent a week or so in hospital but she recovered well and we already had a wonderful little brood anyway. Due to the complications, we decided that Lucy should undergo a sterilisation. The accident two years later of course changed everything, but who could have foreseen that coming over the horizon?

We were not trying to replace Kirsty, and the suggestion by well-meaning family and friends not to do so, was a little annoying, but I suppose sort of understandable, for them. Of course, Kirsty left a huge gap in our lives, and maybe we wanted to fill that gap to some extent, but we really did not analyse it all that much, we certainly did not want a 'stand in' or replacement Kirsty; we knew better than anyone that there could never be another.

The adoption process we underwent was a nightmare from start to finish. Some people may be surprised to learn how bad the system was in the early nineties.

At the time, once adopters were approved, they could approach local authorities to adopt children on the registers. Each month also, we were given a small magazine which contained the photos and brief profiles of the children available for adoption. This was not a book of little babies, most children were over the age of five and almost all were deeply troubled physically or emotionally, often both. Almost none were white children. I am unsure why; it is simply a fact. If I was to guess at a reason it would be that adoption of white babies in perfect health is less difficult a task than adoption of other children with troubles; but I am not a social worker so can only guess.

As it happened, colour, creed and ethnic origin were not issues to us as we were very happy to adopt outside of our own race, ethnicity etc.

Lucy and I, although uncomfortable with the method of 'advertising' the children, used to eagerly read each profile, and every month searched for someone to whom we could offer a loving home and a chance in life. I cannot tell you the number of children we applied to see. Each and every time we got turned down even for consideration because the children were of different ethnic origin to us.

In plain speak, the children were of ethnic minorities (including Irish) and we were classed as 'white British'. The councils did not dress it up, they simply told us as it was, British white parents pretty much could not adopt black children or children from other ethnic minorities. I have no idea if this was policy or just practice but it was the reality.

We applied for children with physical difficulties and several with hearing issues. We tended to apply to see children who might otherwise find it hard to find adoptive parents, plus we thought that given our experience with Eamon we might be ideal. Every time we were tuned down without even having an interview, we were the wrong ethnicity and we were told that.

There will be people who will not believe this account and I don't blame them, we did not believe it, it was the most outright racism I have ever witnessed or was it inverted racism? Who knows? All I know is that it felt wrong. It seemed more important to the authorities to find ethnic matches rather than to lift these poor creatures from a childhood in care.

Misguided ethical theory at the time destroyed lives every day. Ignorant plebs like Lucy and me were roundly criticised for objecting because we were not sophisticated enough to get it! Parents left without adoptive children and children left in care and temporary foster homes.

On one occasion, I asked our trainer why she and other social workers felt it was so bad for a white couple to adopt a black child and she told me, by way of an example simple enough for me to understand, that if the child came home one day complaining of having been racially abused that we, being white, would not be able to identify with that, thus be unable to help the child. I countered that if Eamon came home after being bullied for being disabled (as he occasionally was) should we have to give him up for adoption to a disabled parent? She disliked me anyway but after that the relationship got worse.

Our final effort, and it was a real and genuine effort, was to apply for a family of four siblings. They were all under seven and had various fathers, thus they had various mixed ethnicities, including but not limited to white British. These children had many issues and had almost no chance of ever being adopted unless they were split up as a family. I remember being so optimistic about them. We had the chance to make a real difference to kids who had pretty much no chance from birth. We were told that although the ethnicities did vary and include our own that we were not sufficiently representative of the diversity of the family. We

Father's Day

disengaged with the process that day. I wonder how many others also gave up in the face of such dogma. God, I detest social workers.

Our adventure with IVF started in 1992, in fact to be fair we started before we had given up completely on adoption, we'd suspected for a while it was hopeless.

The NHS did not sponsor fertility treatment at the time, if the family already had a child. Our finances still had not recovered from the accident but we managed to gather up enough loot to cover one cycle. It was not cheap.

One of the biggest issues with IVF and one of the reasons it fails so often is because it is so stressful and stress is not good for pregnancy, any type of pregnancy from conception to birth. Let's face it, stress is not good for anything.

Scraping together a couple of grand and knowing it was our only chance inevitably brought with it stress and along with that a higher risk of failure. I am sure many people will identify with the predicament and will have experienced it. The more the doctors tell you to not stress about things the more you inevitably do.

It was what it was, and we entered the process very optimistically, probably with unrealistic expectations as to the likely outcome. At the time Lucy had about a 30% chance of conceiving and 50% of carrying full term. We knew a thing or two from past experience about odds, and doctors and 30% to us seemed an excellent bet.

The clinic was in a hospital in Bristol and after the first four weeks or so of various daily injections Lucy had three good eggs removed and they all fertilised, and replaced a little while later. It was more than a little disappointing when the cycle failed; the fertilised eggs just did not attach. All those injections, nasal sprays and hope, but we'd been through worse. It was a blow but it was tolerable.

Anyone who undergoes an unsuccessful IVF cycle will tell you that it is sort of addictive, not for the fix but for the possibility of success. As with a crack cocaine habit (I imagine); you find the cash you need to sustain it, no matter what. Somehow, we managed to find more funds but also, we found an IVF charity in Birmingham which agreed to subsidise a single cycle in their clinic. I don't remember the figures but it was going to cost us about 25% of a normal cycle plus the drugs.

Up and down the motorway to the clinic for injections, scans and more injections, I don't remember if it was every day but it seemed that way. Three eggs again and three implants. We did the pregnancy home tests, in spite of them being pointless, due to the artificially high levels of hormones because of the process itself. Alas, as before, the home tests and the clinic confirmed 'no pregnancy'.

It was harder the second time, I can't be sure why, but it was. Incredibly the clinic told us that they would give us another cycle free of charge if we could find the money for the drugs. They knew our history and I figure they perhaps felt sorry for us. We could tolerate the pity if it produced a child, so there was no debate, no question; like the addicts we had become, and we went for another 'hit'.

A few months earlier we'd bought Lucy a little car; an old Vauxhall Chevette. It belonged to a colleague of mine and the cylinder head had blown so I got it for almost nothing. I repaired it and did it up and it made a great run-around for her. It meant I did not have to take time off work every time Eamon visited the hospital, which was often.

It was great to have, but we could at a push do without it, so we sold the car and got enough money for the drugs for one more cycle. By now the whole thing had become a real drain on us, not just financially, but emotionally and physically, particularly for Lucy. This really had to be the last time for more than just reasons of finance. We needed to kick the habit.

From the start it could not have gone more wrong. Half way through the treatment Lucy's IVF surgeon was suspended because of allegations made against him. Lucy had never had any issues with him but apparently some others had. He was eventually struck off so there must have been something to it.

When the time for harvesting came, they found the three eggs now showed as being just two eggs and a substantial growth which was not an egg, it was a cyst. These were not uncommon when so many hormones have been taken over a short period of time but it was a problem.

We were told that the best course was to stop the process and remove the growth as the two eggs were, given their size, not really viable. The alternative was to alter the drugs in such a way as to allow the eggs to remain in the hope that the cyst would go. I'm not sure how it works, but they can hold or suspend the normal cycles by using hormones, and make the body do one thing or the other, as they wish.

The upshot meant extending a changed drug regime for several more weeks. The issue for us was that we simply had no more money for the extended drug programme, we didn't even know for how long it was expected to last.

The clinic spoke to our GP in Dursley and so did Lucy and incredibly and completely without authority to do so, he paid for all the extra drugs necessary. Thus, we continued for the three more weeks.

To avoid daily return trips to Birmingham I had to inject Lucy in her bum cheek twice a day and she had to take an inhaler every four hours around the clock. We bought four alarm clocks to ensure strict compliance.

The cyst stopped growing and Lucy had two eggs which were still just about viable and these were removed after what was effectively a 7-week spell on hormones of various types. A week or so later the fertilized eggs were implanted, both were viable, or they would not have been used, but it was obvious no one was optimistic. We were told that in normal circumstances they would not have tried.

We did not do any home pregnancy tests this time; in fact, we were about as sure as we could be that the cycle was yet another failure. I have to confess that making babies the traditional way was a good deal less stressful and a whole lot more fun.

Something else about our visits to the IVF clinic in Birmingham which sticks in my mind is a little shop I used to visit when Lucy had to be left to the prodding and scanning. Like the clinic, it is closed now. It was an Indian delicatessen and it sold the most incredible samosas.

While Lucy was being tortured for our mutual benefit I was scoffing samosas. Well, a man must do his bit in these things, I guess. We used to take a bag of them home and the thought of that time always stimulates in me a real need to eat vegetable samosas. I fancy one now as I write.

Almost six years later while I was managing fibre optic installations around the UK I worked on that very street and visited that same shop and bought a bag of the delicious triangles and took them home. Lucy, Eamon and I enjoyed them very much; as did our, by then, 5-year-old daughter Megan.

Chapter Thirteen

Quietly Unwell
(2004)

As the time passed, we tried to stay living in Gloucestershire for as long as we could; the continuity for Eamon was important as people there knew him and it was home. Various forces conspired against us however and a move was becoming inevitable.

By 1996 my employer had closed the office in Bristol and relocated to Guildford and Leeds. The company, in consideration for Eamon, had deferred my relocation as long as possible but by 1998 the situation was becoming unmanageable for us due to pressures outside of work.

I was travelling down from Gloucestershire to Guildford to stay in hotels for two or three nights a week or alternatively had to commute considerable distances. Eventually, unable to put it off any longer we reluctantly moved north where I took a position in Project Management in the Leeds office.

We bought a large tired old brick-built house in Bubwith, a beautiful little village in the East Riding of Yorkshire where we spent the next couple of years renovating and extending it. Eamon after the initial bullying in his first school in Yorkshire thrived in the new one and Megan started in the local infant's school. She was a bright but shy little girl and the apple of my eye. The struggle we had to drag her into the world was more than worth it.

Father's Day

By that time although relocated and settled in Yorkshire near to my office the job still took me away from home much more than I wanted. Most weekdays I was in a hotel some place or another, from Edinburgh to Plymouth and most places in-between. I was by then Northern Team Leader in a power and telecoms installation programme. I enjoyed the work which involved overseeing multiple contracts, from conception to completion in towns and cities and on the infrastructure in between.

It was an exceptionally busy and stressful time, partly due to the job but I was also completing my final year of Law School, and renovating the house. It must have been obvious to others but I had not realised at the time that I was ill, and showing signs of the stress. One occasion late in the evening travelling home from Glasgow to Yorkshire I missed my exit from the motorway and had not noticed until I was almost in Preston, some seventy miles after the Penrith exit. There were numerous other examples, of not just loss of concentration but dangerous loss. It affected my decision making and risk taking, and even I began to see this.

On another occasion Megan fell from the climbing bars at school, and broke her arm, so I was rushing back to see her when the police stopped me on the M74. There had been no need to rush of course, but it is what dad's do I suppose, and it was very stupid of me. I was doing 115 MPH so I got a year ban as it was considered dangerous driving in Scotland, which to be fair, it probably was.

The company were really good about it, and did accept that I maybe had a little too much on my plate, so they found me a role in the office, ironically in Guildford, some way from home in Yorkshire or the office in Leeds. I was tasked with re writing all the operating procedures for civils and fibre installations.

It was a task I could partly do remote from the office so I worked from home every Monday. I would travel down to the office by train on Tuesday and return on Friday. I'd stay in the Hog's Back Hotel just outside the town or at The Inn on The Lake in Godalming or the Forte in Guildford, nice enough hotels and, as it was my own fault I could hardly complain.

The company paid for everything, including first class travel on the train. I had a good breakfast on the way down but always skipped a meal homeward bound as we used to take the children to an Italian at home every Friday night.

Lucy and the kids would collect me from the station in York and we'd drive back to Selby. Sometimes we'd go into York but not often as places there tended to be a bit pricey.

Although the event I now wish to recount did not actually happen to me, it is how it did not happen to me which makes me think about circumstance, coincidence and plain good or bad luck. I think about it because obviously, my family and I have had exceptional bad luck in the past;

Father's Day

simply because we were in the wrong place at the wrong time. One tends to remember the bad luck, but often good luck goes unmentioned, simply because we don't know it has occurred.

Had the fire in France happened in the next tent, or on another day, I would have recounted it maybe as an anecdote of a close call or maybe not at all. I recount the following with that in mind, to illustrate that tiny line between a close call and utter catastrophe. A line we probably cross or come close to crossing more often than any of us realise. At 06:12 on Wednesday 28th February 2001 I straddled that line.

I used to get the early train from York down to Kings Cross at 6.02 every Tuesday morning so that after crossing London on the underground I arrived into the office in Guildford before 10:30. One train, two tube rides, and a taxi. Monday morning was out of the question due to how busy it was. I only once ever broke that routine for almost a year.

On Tuesday, February 27th 2001 I had been unwell and decided to take the day off. It was pretty much unheard of for me to miss a day of work due to sickness. I'd informed the office and all was good. The following day, the 28th, still not feeling great I stayed an extra half hour in bed and determined to miss the 06:02 and get a later train down in a couple of hours. This was something also that I had never done before, I have always found getting up early to be very easy. I remember clearly hitting the clock buzzer, turning over and telling Lucy I'd get a later train.

Around 8am as we were getting the kids into the car to take me up to York Station on their elongated school run, my mobile phone and house phone rang at the same time. I picked up and spoke to a colleague, Neil. He told me that the six o'clock train had crashed into a car just south of Selby and that there had been several fatalities. Later I learned that in fact 10 had sadly lost their lives, all of whom had been in the first three carriages, which was where I always sat. It was the worst train disaster for some time in the UK.

At the time it seemed a little surreal. It was only by a remarkable twist that I was due to get on the train a day late in the first place and yet another twist of fate that made me miss it. I wonder had there been a plan for me and that plan changed at the last minute? Of course, I don't wonder that… life is a series of coincidence but I do wonder how close we all come every day from a swerving car, a falling scaffold tube or a wayward cell which turns cancerous.

How many times have any of us walked unknowingly past tragedy simply by making a decision one way or another. Occasionally we can see the effect of our choices like I could with my decision to catch a later train, or to go to France for a holiday. What if in 1984 I had taken another job offered me and not met Lucy? What alternative tragedy or delight would have awaited me? Our

Father's Day

whole lives really do depend upon happenstance I suppose; some good, some not so good.

I suppose in some ways it makes accepting our tragedy a little bearable. No ones' fault, just circumstance and bad luck. I do often contemplate, and I always feel unsettled about how much worse it must be for parents whose children are taken deliberately by some fiend, or who die due to badness of another. How on earth do they ever reconcile themselves with that loss?

The train journeys stopped when I got my driving licence back in late 2001 but not before having to take a re-test. We moved to the other side of Selby late the same year, to a village called Thorpe Willoughby where we found our next home, or more accurately our next renovation project, one in a long line of renovations.

I got my company car back, and I continued to travel around the UK and I missed Lucy and the children desperately and felt guilty being away so often, but on the plus side the money was good, and the job was challenging and rewarding, it could have been a good deal worse, I guess. My employer National Grid could easily have sacked me for losing my licence and that they kept me on at such a cost to them was quite a compliment I suppose.

I'd phone Megan from whatever hotel I was staying and tell her stories of my friends, the wolves that were outside the house looking after her while I was away, or about the princess in the tower I could see from my hotel room, and my contemplations about the possibility of rescue by climbing up her hair. Lucy would call other nights and read to me over the phone.

It was during this period, often away from home, that I had time to contemplate my life, the things gone by and what the future could hold. Maybe it was the first opportunity I had to grieve for Kirsty and maybe it was just because I missed my family but whatever the reason, I could feel change. It worried me a little, it was not good change, it was dark and it was a bit scary.

Unknown to me at the time others, including colleagues, had noticed my mood swings in particular. I became increasingly intolerant of others; I'd always felt disappointed in people but this was more; I was becoming angry at them, angry at everyone, angry at the world.

I felt this immediately after the accident but it had evaporated quite quickly as I supposed, and had been told it would. No one told me it was waiting to get out again however, or how to keep it contained.

I had a busy fast-moving job and often would be called out at night or on weekends due to some issue or another, almost always due to someone not doing their job correctly. I'd get disproportionately annoyed and sacked several people for minor mistakes which inconvenienced me.

I rationalised that for every call down to Plymouth or to London or Cardiff to sort out some problem or other was a call away from my family and I resented the people responsible. It was ridiculous of course; I was very well paid and had a great employer and part of the job description was being 'put upon'.

One of the things I most detested and which really got under my skin were the idiots with whom I would share hotels. Always the same; drinking on expenses and talking loudly to equally vapid idiots about the 'low down torque' on their Ford Mondeo or Audi or some other such bollox they might have read and regurgitated from their motoring magazines; much as a non-football supporter might describe the game as being 'one of two alves', in order to elicit acceptance from others spouting the same vernacular horseshit back to them. They all also seemed, inexplicably, to wear really pointy shoes and shirts with collars of a different colour to the rest of the garment. I have no idea why that should annoy me, but it really, really did, and does.

To me, they were the sort that would always find something in the restaurant about which to make a fuss and thereby demonstrate their refinement and high standards in such matters. Sending back wine and so on whilst demanding the highest of service because no doubt that is what such important people deserve. They were at their worst when in couples or groups where the extraordinary ignorance and discourtesy they displayed seemed to know no bounds.

From my own and Lucy's experience I knew how hard the hospitality business was and how badly paid it was, so such antics used to drive me mad. I had on more than one occasion intervened when guests were being rude to staff and introduced them to my level of rudeness which they could only hope to emulate in their wildest dreams.

It's not that I was looking for fault, it's just that I could not ignore it. Originally, as with most people it was mild annoyance at a useless colleague or a driver who might cut me up in traffic or a rude shop assistant or one of those every day inconveniences we all suffer, but do not dwell upon. I dwelt upon them, in my mind they grew and grew and took on crazy proportions.

From around 2002 or 2003 I had begun to contemplate such things more and more regularly and more and more deeply, particularly when staying away from home and in hotels on business trips. While other businessmen were eyeing up the women in the bar, I was watching how people held their knives or what glass they used for wine. I did begin to wonder if such contemplations were a sign of madness so I must have had some awareness but I had no idea it was bad enough for people to notice.

I was not going around with HB pencils stuck up my nostrils and a pair of underpants on my head saying 'Wibble' as on the famous TV programme but I might as well have.

At the time I greatly enjoyed the actual process of thinking, perhaps too much, I considered it my greatest pastime. I used to wonder, and still do wonder why people list sport or reading or travel as pastimes but no one ever lists thinking or contemplation.

I'd like to say that my contemplations were harmless but they were not. Apart from the self-destruction they were taking up more and more of my time. I pretty much stopped reading books altogether and I must have been very annoying to my colleagues because I would dissect everything and everyone… all the time. I would never let anything drop, I often insulted people deliberately and extremely just because I could and whilst most did deserve it, I was probably behaving like a bully. Using one's brain against someone is like using one's muscles I suppose.

One chap I worked with came into a meeting one day; he was aged about 45, recently divorced and had thinning hair into which he put grease. It was sticking up in the style employed at the time by teenagers, or estate agents. I asked him, in front of everyone, why he had put 'that shit' in his hair. Like I say, he deserved it but I should not have done it, I should have waited until he had turned his back and made fun of him then, as is the usual more socially agreeable way.

No one told me, not even Lucy, though she must have seen it. I was getting worse and worse and although I suppose I knew I was the one out of step it takes a long time for anyone to see fault in one's self, some never do.

We settled into our new home in Thorpe Willoughby and finished remodelling and extending it, as we had done to the last three. I managed a respectable 2:2 in my Batchelor of Laws. A 2:2 is not great I suppose but for a boy unable to read at age 11 and classed as educationally subnormal, not so bad either. I'd proved what I needed to prove academically to others, and to myself.

I started the law degree with huge enthusiasm and vigour but studying for years at the age of almost forty was a struggle. I'd had to do enormous amounts of reading and for me that was a challenge and probably took much longer than it should have.

I noticed also around this time that I was, as I say, reading for leisure a good deal less. Reading was something I used to enjoy. My levels of concentration had fallen away and even a Stephen King, who I always enjoyed, was, for me, hard to finish by 2001.

By mid-2003 Eamon was accepted by Liverpool to study Veterinary Science. Lucy's father had passed away in the February from a stroke or a 'scratch' as Megan called it and my father died in the April as the result of falling from a ladder.

He was 73, had been a Royal Navy deep sea diver, an explosives expert who worked in the most treacherous waters in the world, and yet died from falling off the fourth rung of a ladder when cleaning out gutters in his home in Ireland. It's as I say, chance; wrong place, wrong time.

I had only spoken to my father and mother a few times since the accident thirteen years earlier, not at all in the eight years before he died. The death was sad but not unduly so. Death is always sad I suppose, in different ways. I'd considered not going to the wake but Lucy persuaded me it would be for the best. It was the second time I'd been back to Ireland since leaving eighteen years previously. My mother and sister made it clear that Lucy was not welcome, and given the woman had just lost her husband, it would have been difficult to argue the ridiculous prohibition, though I was tempted. I took Eamon with me.

The wake was a typically Irish affair. People who hardly knew my father expressing sorrow at the loss. It was an open casket and I found the experience more upsetting than I had anticipated. Why do people try to elicit public displays of grief? I wonder. I find them as unpleasant as public displays of affection. Leaving the casket open for a day in the front room was not in my opinion a good thing but for once, my dad was not in control.

I loved my father, and I know that he loved me. That I suppose never goes in spite of what happens over a lifetime. I did not feel the need to declare it to one and all, nor did he.

The priest turned up and I wished I had something sharp. The night of the wake I went to bed early with Eamon in my sister's room. Will, Roger and Edward stayed up late drinking and arguing loudly. I was glad to be out of it, and for once also glad for Eamon's hearing impairment.

The funeral itself was in Wales and I accompanied the body back on the ferry. For all his loyalty to 'The Homeland' my father wanted to be buried in the UK. It was the last time I saw my brother Edward, and the last time the family would be together. As I say, I had considered not going due to the way Lucy had been, and continued to be treated but I concluded, correctly, that it was probably for the best.

The experience was all the more remarkable because at the time I was at my most hypomanic and critical of everything. I had not yet been diagnosed but even I knew something was not right, and ironically that is partly why I made such an effort to do the right thing with the funeral. Sometimes when you know something is not right the compensations you make can more than make up for the issue, so things don't just appear normal, they appear better than normal.

The brothers had all grown up and gone their own ways, other than Brandon, the eldest, who remained in close touch as did Mike, the youngest, to a lesser extent. Most seemed content to keep their distance from me and vice versa. The band of brothers was no more I suppose, but all things come to an end and other things begin.

The significant events of 2003 did not end with the funeral. A few weeks later Lucy and I shared a BBQ with some friends in Selby, and in some drink inspired plan we all decided to immigrate to Romania where, according to some TV programme, property was cheap and life apparently was good.

In the cold light of the next day our friends had changed their minds about leaving the UK, presumably because they were sober. Lucy and I, also sober (she has never been drunk) had within three months sold up and immigrated, not to Romania… we were after all not rash and impulsive… but to France.

Chapter Fourteen

France - Part 1
2003

Lucy had noticed changes in me for a while before the move to France, though I had not noticed her noticing. My quickness to anger and irritability in particular but she had not said anything. I was annoyed with the situation mostly because I thought that in time it would pass or improve but it did not, and even the move to France had not made much of a difference; if anything, I was even more intolerant of others, but we were so busy I suppose it got sort of buried or excused.

I have always been a little hyper but I was gradually getting worse and I never seemed to come down, or if I did it was not for long. I was 'over the top' with everything. I'd managed to conceal it to some extent or to excuse it. Excusing it was easy enough while doing the law degree, the job, and the renovations and so on.

When we sat around the barbeque that June evening the plan to emigrate from the UK was just a drunken idea. It had not been something we'd specifically thought about before that night, but when the idea of starting afresh in a new country had been mooted it was embedded in my mind and it was going to happen. This is just how I was at that time.

We'd disposed of the idea of Romania partly due to the fact that it was too much of an unknown and the language issue would have been huge. I had the remnants of French from when I was a child and we both loved what we thought French rural life had to offer.

Megan was just nine, but already impressed by the piercings and tattoos sported by the plethora of pouting teens on TV and everywhere else in the UK, and that terrified us. French children it seemed dwelled in their childhood longer whereas British children wanted to grow into teenagers way too soon, and that French or European appreciation of childhood also appealed to us both.

At work I'd been shoe-horned into the procurement department as a senior contracts officer. I was unwelcome and where I did not want to be. Several of the staff seemed to resent me coming in above them, and gave no consideration to why.

The house was just about finished too and prices in the UK were once again on the up. The time seemed right.

The four of us travelled to Bergerac and we spent a week driving around meeting various agents from Bordeaux almost down to Toulouse. The feeling of loading the kids into the car and setting off for the ferry was a little unsettling but the distraction of Eamon and Megan arguing in the back seat soon took our minds off the subject.

The meetings and property viewings were prearranged and although there was a good deal of driving, we viewed over a dozen places. The properties were woeful and not what we had expected.

The last two days were promised to Eamon and Megan as rest days and so it was that on a Saturday afternoon, we found ourselves sitting for lunch on a little pavement café in the town of Sainte-Foy-la-Grande. Opposite, over the square, was the inevitable French Estate Agency, the Immobilier. Lucy, who found walking past an Estate Agent as difficult for her as it was for my father to walk past a pub, excused herself as she wandered over to take a look in the window.

Ten minutes later I paid the bill and followed her, with Eamon and Megan complaining and trailing behind. As we approached Lucy was coming out of the office with a leaflet in her hand.

'Window Shopping normally doesn't include going into the shop' Eamon suggested to his mother. She'd laughed and showing the three of us the brochure she said;

'Well, it's a pity to come all this way and not see one more'.

I of course agreed and the other two groaned at the inevitability.

'Besides we have a viewing tomorrow' she beamed.

Lucy had actually managed to arrange an accompanied Sunday viewing of a set of buildings nearby. We deduced that the sellers were 'keen', as nobody did anything on a Sunday in France.

We met the agent at the gates of the property. It was situated in a tiny hamlet on the outskirts of the village of Montcaret, in the department of the Dordogne almost exactly half way between Bordeaux and Bergerac.

We had to that date bought five homes, each of which we had decided upon before seeing inside. So it was with 'Le Petit Borie'.

As we entered the gateway and parked Lucy said;

'I love it' and I replied;

'It's the one', and that was that.

The agent and the owners and later the notaire were amazed at how swiftly we made our offer, and proceeded with the purchase. They were used to the Brits turning up and on impulse deciding to buy and even signing preliminary contracts only later in the cold light of day changing their minds, often outside the cooling off period, and sometimes losing their substantial deposits which though unpaid at signing, were due. There were lawyers in France whose sole occupation was chasing such deposits for disappointed but soon to be enriched French clients.

The property consisted of three ancient stone buildings sitting in about one and a half acres of land. A little stone cottage with three bedrooms, a smaller stone cottage or gite; don't ask me the difference, and a massive stone barn, connected to the cottage.

The place was relatively secluded but within a short drive of Castillon-la-Bataille to the west and Sainte-Foy-la-Grande to the east with Bergerac and the airport less than thirty minutes away and the river Dordogne under a kilometre as the crow flies.

The cottage was habitable though basic and the two-bedroom gite, which the previous owners had started to renovate, was pretty much habitable too. The largest of the buildings was a two hundred square metre stone barn, at least 300 years old. It was perfect for what we wanted.

The house in Yorkshire sold quickly and without event and coincided within a week of completion on the French property. I arranged for a three month leave of absence with my employer and by September 2003, after spending a week in a hotel in Sainte-Foy-la-Grande with all our belongings in storage we moved into the cottage.

That first week saw the most tremendous thunder and lightning storm we had ever seen.

Eamon by now had a start date for university in Liverpool, and he'd worked out he could fly to Bordeaux and be 'home' within ninety minutes, which was faster than if we were in Yorkshire. When I returned to work from my leave of absence I could fly from Bordeaux to Heathrow or Bergerac to Stanstead and be in Yorkshire three hours later.

It was very straight forward, easy and remarkably inexpensive. Initially I used the Stanstead to Bergerac route on Ryanair, a faster and cheaper route but I think I am one of the few who actually meant it when I said 'never again'. British Airways charged a little more but they treated passengers like humans and not animals.

Father's Day

The first months in France were hectic, Eamon stayed for three weeks before disappearing off to university. Megan started school where, after an initial phase of crying every night and telling us how much she hated us, she soon grasped the language and settled in with a bunch of new friends. She was the only English speaker in her school so had to learn the language very quickly.

I should say that although she did learn very fast it was a very challenging time for Megan or 'Reebot' as I know her. A new country, a new language, culture and so on.

Although a very timid child Megan always displayed an extraordinarily advanced sense of right and wrong, even as a child. On one occasion, maybe a few months into school in France she witnessed a younger girl being bullied on the school bus. The girl, who was Greek, and the daughter of a GP had learning issues, and several of the older local boys were teasing her. Megan stood up and scolded the boys as best she could in her new language, and they apparently immediately retreated, and other children joined Megan in her protests… but it was she and she alone saw the injustice and stood up against it, in spite of being crushingly shy.

Another example of her sense of empathy was displayed when she was ten. We had been in France a year or so and were on holiday in Havana visiting a cigar factory. All the workers were lined up on their school-desk stations working away, a man at the top of the room read to them from the newspaper. The place was hot and humid… oppressive, but everyone seemed happy.

Megan pulled at my arm and was crying and I picked her up, checking to see if she had snagged herself on a nail or burned herself or somehow otherwise hurt herself. I asked:

'what's the matter' and she explained that she was crying because she felt so sorry for the workers. She was 10 and had a capacity for empathy I have rarely seen in an adult. Words fail me when I try to express how proud I am of her.

When the Covid crisis hit in 2020 she by coincidence a week before had given up her job translating and taken one for a considerably lower salary working for a charity helping women with mental health issues making the transition from institutions back to society… all the time working also for a homeless charity in Bristol. She has always been this way.

My apologies for the slight digression, but that is a little about our little 'replacement'.

Back to the place in France: The plan had been to renovate the two cottages with a view to offering them as holiday lets and to convert the barn into the main dwelling for the family. At the time I intended continuing to work for my employer in the UK and to commute and to that end I also rented a little cottage in Selby. I was planning to give it two years and then finish with the job. I was sure I could manage the travelling for that short time and hopefully the ever-recurring redundancy round would land conveniently for me. My leave of absence from work in the UK began in late September and was due to end immediately after Christmas of 2004.

We used local Artisans for the two big jobs which needed doing, and got them underway almost immediately. The search for a builder with all the requisite skills to do everything else proved impossible. From local artisans who thought it impossible, to the expat British so-called builders who knew less about building than Megan did. Two months were wasted before we realised there was only one way to do it, and that was to do it ourselves.

The three months long leave of absence evaporated pretty quickly but by the time I returned to work we had a leak free roof on each of the buildings and beautifully re pointed stone walls. Lucy and I had also managed to make the cottage more than comfortable with a large wood burner in the living room, which was handy because that winter was the coldest in twenty years with snow four inches thick on the ground for a week or so.

Initially, after returning to work, I came home weekends and worked on the project day and night. While I was away Lucy erected stud partition, laid tiles and demolished and decorated. Perhaps one day such an enterprise could make a never-ending TV programme…?

One Monday, sixteen ton of sand was delivered to the front of the house and she, all five foot two of her, had by the following Friday moved the entire mound by shovel and wheel barrow to the back of the property, ready for me on the Friday afternoon to start mixing mortar and building.

Each return trip I made would find hundreds of concrete blocks lifted by Lucy and carried to the point of use, many up ladders, ready for me to build and not waste time carrying.

I easily made it home most weekends and with judicious use of my holidays I could take most Fridays and some Mondays as leave. It was not at all unusual and on Fridays the plane was full of similar commuters. It worked really well, and in fact I spent less time commuting each week from France to the UK than I used to from Yorkshire to Guildford.

By now I detested my job. In fact, I had hated it before the leave of absence, mainly due to my enforced transfer to the Procurement Department. In addition, a new tranche of clueless managers had evolved while I had been away; they used the 'synergy' word and the 'paradigm' word which they had picked up on some management training day and would drop into reports and conversations, much as I suppose, one day in the future, contestants on a show called 'The Apprentice' might.

I wanted to strangle them each time I encountered the dreadful creatures. Alas they were my managers and strangulation, like so many similar reasonable activities, would have fallen foul of the new politically correct rules, with which everyone was so obsessed.

It wasn't just the job though. We'd moved to France in part to help me settle. My mood swings had not improved however. By the time I was back in the office things were a lot worse. I found my ability to tolerate people just about nil and I know it was not their fault, it was mine, in fact I knew it at the time. Although clearly something was wrong it never occurred to me or to Lucy or indeed to my managers and colleagues that I actually was suffering from a diagnosable mental health problem and it urgently needed addressing.

Thankfully I had the remnants of self-awareness, and I knew I was the one out of step, and getting worse, so I finally sought help from my General Practitioner in early 2004. She informed me of the long waiting time for appointments with psychiatrists but added me to the list anyway. Exhibiting my usual inability to wait for anything I arranged to see a private consultant psychiatrist in Harrogate, and got an appointment almost immediately.

At the first consultation he kept me waiting five minutes so I left. I later phoned the clinic and explained that I would happily wait in an NHS clinic, but when I was paying good money, I was not about to wait. I was such an arsehole, but sort of had a point. The shrink actually agreed with me, and arranged my next appointment, at which I was not kept waiting. I'd considered turning up late but thought better of it.

The consultation was for forty minutes and when it concluded the doctor informed me that he had rarely seen a more classic case of Bi Polar Effective Disorder. I did not even know what the condition was, and when I got home and looked it up, I realised that the symptoms might easily have been written for me.

A month or two later the NHS appointment came through and the diagnosis was confirmed by another shrink. Both also concluded that I was suffering from PTSD, which, with hindsight, I suppose was sort of inevitable.

I'm going to talk now a little about the illness and how it affected me. This is a personal perspective and not reflective of everyone with the illness but certainly many sufferers will see things they recognise. The illness manifests in its own way in most sufferers, but there are common themes.

First, the cause: No one knows this for sure, but it is widely accepted that a combination of environmental and genetic issues underpin the illness and that 'triggers' cause it to manifest, or activate. That is to say that a group of the population has the disposition for the illness but not necessarily the illness itself.

I find a useful comparison is the physical illness of cancer, where it is known that a person can live a long life with the disposition to develop the illness but never actually get ill. A crude comparison maybe but a fair one, I think.

Triggers typically are serious and stressful life events, particularly from childhood. The NHS lists the following examples: Physical or sexual abuse, the death of a family member or loved one, divorce etc. You get the point?

Bi Polar is a very complicated illness and its range of symptoms is vast. Few sufferers exhibit all the symptoms, some of which I shall mention in a moment. The main characteristic, suggested by the name, is a swing from one mood, depressive to the opposite mood; mania, and everything between. It's basically a mood disorder, the extremes of which can be catastrophic.

Most sufferers do not go to full blown mania or indeed full depression. To further complicate matters depression often manifests in behaviours which are easily confused with mania or hypomania (a milder form of mania).

The symptoms, or how the illness manifests are many but in the depressive phase include: Loss of energy but inability to sleep: Feelings of worthlessness and guilt, self-loathing, which can be overwhelming: extreme melancholy or sadness for no reason; suicidal thoughts. The severity of these symptoms varies wildly from person to person and depending on what phase of the illness they are enduring.

People suffering from Bi Polar are 30 time more likely to commit suicide than are non-sufferers. This is not meant to shock you, it is, as I see it, a startling exposition of an illness all but ignored by society until the last 20 years. One I remind the reader, for which I was sacked by my employer after 21 years of loyal service. I did not plan to get it and did nothing at all to cause it. We shall come to that.

So, we have looked at the depressive side let's look at the manic side. People tend to think of depression negatively and mania as less so; sufferers while manic certainly do not see it as a down side at all. Sadly, they are mistaken; huge damage is often done in these 'high' states.

Whilst some sufferers (me included) are aware of the impropriety of much of their behaviour while high, they simply cannot stop it. Think Tourette's if you find that hard to believe.

Manic type symptoms include; an extreme increase in energy, with fast moving thoughts, out of control feelings, much as if drugs have been taken; inability or lack of desire to sleep, I often got by on less than 4 hours at my worst; impulse behaviours, this includes such things as reckless sexual behaviour, reckless spending, dangerous behaviours, criminal activity, verbal abuse… deciding to immigrate to France on a whim; racing thoughts and speech, speaking extremely quickly, jumping from topic to topic, or no longer making sense to anyone but themselves.

I think this is the characteristic I most obviously display when ill. Also included is the strange but very definite inclination to be overly generous, some sufferers giving away all their possessions for example.

The above just touches on the nature of the illness and whilst I am loathe to add positives to an illness such as this it would be wrong not to mention what some sufferers report as positive.

We all know that sufferers tend to take on grandiose plans and ideas with little hope of success. We also know that some sufferers do actually succeed in their plans, plans they might never have considered had they not been Bi Polar in the first place.

Many sufferers attribute their creativity to the illness and indeed many experts agree. It is a dangerous thing however to indulge such an illness and risk the catastrophe that can happen, just for a little payback by way of creativity.

I'm going to write a memoir. Is that an overly ambitious or grandiose task? You tell me… you're reading it. I was ESN and yet wrote a novel, a good one according to reviewers. Was that grandiose or was it realistic? I don't mean to sound facetious; I honestly do not know. I am sure that many of the things I have archived have been informed partly by my illness, and many of my failures too… but who can tell which? Does it matter even?

My illness is well controlled now, and has been for years, mainly thanks to lithium which is the primary treatment for mood disorders such as Bi Polar. I take it every evening and it has massively improved my quality of life, and those around me, yet no one knows how lithium actually works on the brain. Hard to believe isn't it. Well try this for hard to believe:

Over 13 billion years ago when the universe was born there were only three elements formed by the Big Bang. There was hydrogen, there was helium and there was one more element. It was not carbon, as you might suppose or any of the other 118 odd elements; it was lithium. Yes, lithium is more ancient by billions of years than even carbon, the building block of our planet and everything on and in it. It was one of the first three things to exist.

Don't worry; I am not getting a grandiose idea. lithium existed for billions of years but was only discovered in 1817 by August Arfvedson. Yet, it was being used to treat manic behaviour by the ancient Greeks and Romans.

It is extremely well documented that people exhibiting excited behaviour and alternating moods were treated to long baths in hot springs in both these ancient civilisations. Unknown to them the hot springs had exceptionally high levels of lithium; and it worked!

Lithium as a drug for treating mental illness was not actually used knowingly until as late as 1949, having previously been used to dissolve uric acid, thus help with gout.

Back to my illness, and how it manifested in me. So now, with hindsight, I can see that a good deal of my own behaviour was very clearly due to Bi Polar, and some of it was due to me being an idiot and a human. I hate the Hollywood habit of excusing all bad behaviour with suspect Bi Polar diagnosis by very well-paid doctors in the Hills.

Almost all major decisions I make these days I double check, and even run by some other trusted

Father's Day

person. OK I admit the 1968 Jaguar Mk 2 was a surprise to Lucy as was the Harley Davidson but what can I say? I'm a bloke!

When I was first diagnosed, I sort of let the illness run wild for a time. Not deliberately, and to be fair, on several occasions behaviours absolutely due to the illness have not been fairly attributed to it.

It was a shock of course to know that I had a serious mental disorder, but in a way also a relief, in fact a massive relief. The doctor explained that while it could not be cured the condition could be managed with drugs and therapy. It was not so much finding out the problem could be managed that made me feel better; it was the fact that I really had a chemical imbalance which made me the arse I knew I had been for so long. What a relief; maybe I was not an arse after all… I sort of didn't like who I was at that time and so I was very optimistic. Seeking help was the best thing I had done in years. If anyone reading this feels maybe they are misfiring… go see someone, pay if you must, it is worth it.

I saw the psychiatrist regularly after the diagnosis and, as mentioned, I was put onto Lithium Carbonate, which did help with the mood swings but it took a long time. I was still very hypomanic and if I am honest a little out of control. I was drinking too much, spending too much and doing everything I did usually but way too much, but things were getting better, for sure.

I suppose in some ways when one gets to the root of the problem and starts to deal with it, things get a little worse before they get better. It was that way for me. I can't imagine how annoying I must have been for my colleagues. Well, I sort of can, as they were continually complaining to my manager, Peter, about me. The complaints fell on open ears because Peter did not like me one bit, and made little attempt to conceal it.

It was around this time that two things happened which although they turned out to be connected were not intended to be, not by me anyway. The first thing was that a round of redundancies was announced by my employer and the company was looking for volunteers, particularly in my department.

I approached my manager and suggested that I might be included, which would have meant I'd have got a small redundancy package and about 15 years later, a small pension of about one fifth of my salary.

I was only about forty-three years old at the time. It would have been a difficult struggle to survive solely on the income from the holiday cottages but one for which Lucy and I were prepared. I could always find other work of course.

I knew that if I wanted redundancy Peter would bust a gut stopping me, but it was only via him that I could apply. Before asking for it I had already approached the Occupational Health Department and kept them apprised of my diagnosis, treatment and prognosis. They agreed to pay my medical fees and at that level were very supportive. Sick absences also were much easier to explain and manage if Occupational Health were involved, that was the main reason I involved them.

Due to the exceptional sensitivity, and at my request, my manager was kept out of the loop, so to speak, regards much of the detail. It was unusual to keep a line manager out of the loop but this was pretty much unchartered territory to the people involved and, unknown to me at the time, dismissal was a real possibility and their preferred option, but they needed to get it right.

Occupational Health, who were very kind, sent me to two external occupational therapist consultants, and this is where the second factor came about. Both of the consultants recommended ill health retirement. I think if my employer had even suspected this would be the case they'd never have sent me. Ill health retirement had not even crossed my mind at the time, nor theirs, I guess. It was almost impossible to qualify for consideration.

Within a day or so of discovering I was being considered for ill health retirement I wrote to my manager withdrawing my request for voluntary redundancy. I put the letter into the internal mail system.

The very same day and clearly before he had opened his post, Peter handed me an envelope which contained a letter refusing me redundancy. He made some comment about the company needing me to stay, which he and a few 'fellow colleagues' seemed to find amusing.

It was highly unusual because I was a prime candidate for redundancy due to my job having already evaporated. I was being paid way over the grade for the role I had been dropped into in the meantime. Getting rid of me would have been something of a coup for a manager. I should have been the first to go on redundancy, and everyone knew it.

Of course, getting ill health retirement was almost impossible, and I was just as likely to get sacked with nothing for non-performance. People seem to think an employer can't do that. They most certainly can, in fact if I remember correctly when I was let go the wording on the letter was 'Incapability' and the procedure used was the 'Incapability Procedure'.

I should perhaps explain the significance of ill health retirement over redundancy. If I was made redundant, I would, as said, get a small redundancy payment and then a very small pension, starting about 15 years later. If on the other hand I was retired on ill health grounds I would be entitled to a much better deal including an immediate tax-free lump sum, and a full pension of half salary, which would commence immediately; index linked with spousal benefits and for life.

Basically, the difference between living comfortably and having no income for 15 years other than the rental from the cottages, which at that time were not even complete.

Incredibly, for reasons at which I can only guess, I was refused even the redundancy package, and the company decided to let me go, but without a pension in place. The worst of all worlds I suppose.

After 21 years of service, I had developed a mental illness and my employer decided I should be sacked. They had the chance to let me go for a deferred and tiny pension, and decided against even that.

So, it was decided, that I was not entitled to redundancy or an ill health retirement pension. Think about how that was for us. I did not ask to be ill. I had been over twenty years with the company and had maybe three days sick in that time, before I got ill. I had been diagnosed with PTSD and Bi Polar Disorder, diagnosed by a total of three psychiatrists and the company's own Occupational Health Consultants recommended ill health retirement. I clearly was very unwell and I was trying to get better. I was declared unable to do the job, by the company itself, and they did not try to find me alternative work.

The decision to sack me was the company's and had nothing to do with the pension trust. The trust refused my ill health pension application and that decision, apparently had nothing to do with the company. Very nice set up, neither responsible for me having no income.

I wonder if in 2022 a company could do such a thing as they did to me then, as they tried to do that is.

Of course, being sacked with no pension was not ideal so in 2004 I compiled an appeal… I had no help from my so-called union (Prospect) or from the company, no help from anyone. Just me, an apparently unemployable mentalist, against the pension fund of the largest utility company in the world, who had already nailed their colours to the mast, so to speak. I was at the time really not well, but in a good way. I knew the odds were stacked against me, but I also knew I had been treated badly.

It was early 2005 when I had the telephone call from the trustees to inform me of the appeal decision, which was in my favour. I was in the middle of laying floor tiles in the barn in France, I had just mixed a batch of adhesive and Lucy was fourteen foot up a scaffold repairing a window. I aimed and almost hit her with the champagne cork from twenty foot. The adhesive set in the bucket as we and Megan got dressed and headed for the Le Péché Mignon at Montazeau for dinner. In spite of the cold, we sat on the terrace overlooking the vineyards eating duck and drinking wine. I got verrrraaayyy drunk.

A little while later I was summoned back to the UK for a meeting with Human Resources. They hired a hotel room in Birmingham, a safe distance from the office and any possibility of me running into colleagues. But word of their spectacular own goal and my 'retirement' was already out. I actually got several cards congratulating me. I am still not sure if they were sent sarcastically or not.

My Team Leader was there, a lovely man named Neil, so was a lady from Human Resources and my manager. The meeting was short and I was asked if I was agreeable to the terms. I made a pretence of considering them and then removed the Human Resources woman's arm from the shoulder... metaphorically of course. She even asked what day I thought would be best for my retirement to begin, I selected my 44th birthday, which was imminent.

I know I sound unforgiving, and yes, of course I gloat a little, but for over a year my family faced the prospect of almost no income simply because I got ill and did not know how to manage. I feel that they should have helped, not discarded me.

Just to be clear; the pension trust did not grant me a pension out of benevolence, they did it because they had no choice, they just needed reminding of the immorality of their initial, default decision.

For almost all of my twenty years with my employer they were exemplary, particularly when we lost Kirsty, they were unbelievably good to us. I think the contrasting way they managed my illness is indicative of the new breed at the time coming up the ranks. Not the old boys, the engineers who could talk engineering and history and art or philosophy and do a great job.

These new types learned what they had to learn to do the job and they did what it took to get up the ladder. They had never read a book or written a poem or learned a single thing which was not required for their progress up the ranks. What ever happened to well-rounded people? I don't mean rotund; I mean complete human beings.

The manager was gone from the company a short time later, and none of my ex-colleagues can say why or where he went. I was of course pleased he'd been my boss, because a different manager might have given me the redundancy, and I would have taken it.

By the summer of 2005 we were open for business, letting the two cottages and living in the almost completed barn. We'd installed a heated swimming pool ourselves, me excavating and Lucy driving the huge dumper truck.

Partly due to my new medication and probably also due to the stress of work being removed and having a very secure financial situation for the rest of our lives, my mood swings levelled off and whilst I remained always a little hypomanic it was and is manageable and even a characteristic which some others enjoy and it certainly accounted for my relentless energy working on the property and any other projects I undertook, including, dare I say; writing.

Chapter Fifteen

France – Part 2

I suppose if I wanted to write a memoir about our move to France and our lives there for 6 or 7 years I could, there is a lot of material. On the one hand I need to mention France as it is an important part of this story, but on the other, do you really want to read *7 years in Montcaret*? Actually, that is a catchy title… maybe one day if no one else thinks of anything similar I shall write such a book!

In the previous chapter for example I covered us building a pool with just a single line. Clearly there was a good deal more to it than that. I was tempted to write about meeting the mayor, getting planning permission and then the construction, mass concrete, reinforcing the walls, slump tests, fitting the liner and importing the heating system from the USA, and so on.

Alas, too many books have been written about such things and for non-readers there are the TV programmes to watch such adventures. Personally, I love such programs.

So, I shall spare you all that. I would like however to mention just a little about our experience.

France was an interesting and eye-opening experience. Once the novelty of the new people, the location and the weather wore off, which took about three weeks, the realisation of just what a daunting and frankly grandiose task we had undertaken dawned on us. More on Lucy than on me because my enthusiasm, I have to admit, was at the time probably partly a symptom of my illness, of which we were initially unaware.

It was a challenge to find any locals willing to undertake the main works. The roofer was relatively easy in comparison and we were glad to get at least that underway. I'd done a little roofing on previous renovations but nothing on this scale and in spite of my over confidence and ambition, even I knew it was too much for me. The scaffolding alone had to wrap the barn and the cottage; it was a huge job which had not been done for well over a hundred years.

Pretty much all of the walls, externally and internally were in a poor state and needed the old lime mortar removed and replaced and we were lucky enough to find an excellent local man to do the work. We had been driving through Pessac one morning and saw a building being re pointed and stopped to have a look. The guy in charge was a lovely man and we exchanged details but it would be almost eighteen months before he could even look at the job. They say it is a good sign if you have to wait for a builder because only bad builders are not busy.

By a stroke of luck, a job he had been due to start fell through and he was able to start as soon as the scaffolding was removed from the roof works. We were naïve as to the amount of work needed and by the time all the old lime mortar was removed, the entire building sand blasted and then repointed much of the garden had disappeared under tons of sand and lime mortar. The result however was absolutely fantastic. A magazine for expats came and did a feature on the buildings and on us, I think they called it a lifestyle piece.

It was by this time that I was returning to work in the UK, as I mention in the last chapter. We redoubled our efforts to find builders to convert the barn into a home. We spoke to several French builders who simply 'did not do that kind of work'. Anyone who has visited rural France will have noted the plethora of bungalows springing up, often within a few yards of beautiful old tumble-down buildings. At the time the French just did not seem to know what they had. The ever-increasing flux of Brits did however and the number of expats renovating was huge.

Partly as a consequence many British builders were easy to be found in the local watering holes. I say 'builders' in the very loosest sense. There were some good guys of course, but the vast majority were 'monkey see monkey do' labourers who could hardly get work on the shovel in the UK, but came to the Dordogne and were suddenly 'Master Builders'.

We interviewed at least six and within moments of speaking to them could see they were utterly clueless, dangerous even. Many so-called electricians for example had no idea of the French regulations and regularly simply imported British cable, switchgear, socket etc. along with their monthly trips for Heinz beans and Tetley tea bags. This almost certainly breached the local regulations, in terms of electrical safety, not cuisine, though that too maybe.

It would not have been so bad if they'd followed UK installation regulations, at least the systems would have been safe, if not compliant, but they mostly did not even know of the existence of regulations, British or French.

It is easy to get an electrical system to work; the correct design is more about how it goes wrong however, not how it works.

I could spot such bad workers and workmanship, any competent person could, but worryingly most people could not. Some of these so-called tradesmen have installed countless dangerous and non-compliant systems all over France.

I should mention by way of fact and not of boastfulness that my first degree from Ireland was in construction and covered in great depth the theory and practice in the system of building, domestic and commercial, from bending moments and design of steel beams to the sizing of sewage pipes and most things in between.

In addition, as I renovated various buildings over the years, I obtained formal qualifications to keep up with changes in regulations. I qualified as a certified electrician, was a member of the Chartered Institute of Plumbing and Heating Engineers, was an OFTEC qualified oil boiler and oil tank installer, inspector and commissioner and qualified to work on pressurised hot water systems (BPEC). So, to be fair, not without some ability in terms of renovation.

The Law degree also helped an appreciation of how important it was to stick to the rules. I did not work for anyone, other than ungrateful family and friends in these capacities, and undertook what training and certification I needed simply for my own benefit, to enable me to safely and competently renovate our own projects. The money it cost in training I have saved many times over not having to employ tradesmen.

Not everyone can be expert, or even be knowledgeable in everything necessary to renovate, but some understanding is required and without it, people run risks they do not even know exist. There is always a cowboy builder ready to exploit any deficiency in knowledge they might detect.

If I remember correctly, we had given up on the idea of employing an expat builder before we had given up on the local French artisans. With the exception of the excellent roofer and equally excellent builder who pointed the walls.

It was exhausting even to get trades to look at the job. Pointing and roofing were standard things, conversion of a barn into a house was not I suppose.

By January or maybe February 2004 we decided we'd do all the work ourselves. When I say 'all', I mean all of it; building of internal foundations, walls, beams to first floor, floorboards plumbing, first and second fix carpentry, electrics, windows, floor tiling, wall tiling, four bathrooms, four bedrooms and so on.

We put in a huge stone fireplace with a new chimney constructed all the way up through the roof, and as mentioned, we even built a salt water heated swimming pool. My first and last, it was 11m long and 4.5m wide and I used to swim 1km in it every morning. Photos of it and the place are online.

It amuses me often when I watch TV programmes and so called 'self-builders' who pay an architect £30k and then turn up to site once a week to interfere, and show off their great taste and 'quirkiness' and then bugger off for another week and claim to have built something.

You know if you have self-built something fifteen years later when you can't move for arthritis in the shoulder or when you can't straighten all your fingers. God preserve us from self-important women on a career break, thinking they are project managing because they have chosen stair carpet or bi-frigging-fold-doors, 'which really do frame the scene' and 'bring the inside out' or 'the outside in' or some other such nonsense. Another tab of Lithium required!

By early 2005 we were putting the finishing touches to the barn and we were exhausted, but as happy as could be. I'd made the most of my sick leave before leaving my career and my shrink had told me that keeping busy was good for me, perhaps I took him a little too literally.

Father's Day

Making friends in France was relatively easy, though I confess I am not a great believer in the notion of friends. I find with few exceptions that people are disappointing. However; I made an effort and within just weeks we met various people of all backgrounds and nationalities.

Many British people moving to France or to other countries protest that they do not want to mix with British ex-pats. They are the same people who visit only the 'untouched' regions of Spain or Greece on their EasyJet package holidays and seek the 'real experience' and read abridged classics, one page per book… just enough to fool anyone who had not read the real thing. They are a mixed lot but can be fairly categorised as 'fakes'; much like the sorts who don't watch TV except for David Attenborough and the news… BBC of course.

We have all met them and no one ever calls them out for what they are. Having Bi Polar I found gave me a certain freedom to do exactly that. It's not an excuse, I did not do it for any reason other than I thought it, and it was true. God will forgive me; he (or she, or it, or they) owes me one. Lucy and I were open to meeting anyone but avoided most if we could. We enjoy Coronation Street and never read anything abridged.

Many of the ex-pats were awful, often on third and fourth marriages 'getting away' from the UK. You can always tell them… over affectionate with each other in public and always considering each other's opinion… just a tad too much.

There were some nice people, as much as I hate to admit such things exist. One or two had a good deal in common with us but were people who we might never otherwise have met.

I had struck up a friendship with an ex-army officer named Ben; an unlikely friendship, for me, but the sort of unlikely friendship which occurred with ex-pats. We met when having a drink in the local Brit watering hole, a very nice little café run by a lovely family who moved into the area at the same time as us.

Ben was doing his best to run an agency showing around prospective British house buyers but it was not going well. It was not at all unusual for expats to try their hand at such things; never allowing their complete lack of the local language or indeed knowledge of property impede them.

Ben had done well; he was from an ordinary background and made the rank of lieutenant colonel in the army in spite of not having a plum in his mouth. His accent, for a man from South Shields, was however painfully practiced and he worked just a bit too hard on it. A particular characteristic which irritated me was the man's insistence on not pronouncing the aspirate 'H'. He had, more likely than not, heard some buffoon in his mess or some other place, where such idiocy is practiced, and not challenged, pronouncing 'a Hotel' as 'an Otel' and taking this to be correct, as so many do, presumed that to drop the letter 'H' from all words would doubly reinforce the perception of sophistication. Thus, he would drop the 'H' almost all the time and ended up sounding like a posh cockney with a speech impediment, like something out of a Noel Coward film.

People dropping their 'H's never bothered me normally; many UK regional accents would not be what they are without a shortage of aspirated 'H's. It was only when it was done in some attempt to impress that it annoyed me; I dislike affectation in all its forms but most particularly the ill-informed variety, which is its most common manifestation.

Another trait which Ben had was that when he met what he thought were 'the lower orders' of which he originally had thought us to be, he would often start the conversation with racism or sexism. It was shocking, more so because he was neither a racist nor a sexist. No doubt when speaking to squaddies it worked, heck it might even have been on the young 'hofficer's' training manual on 'how to speak to enlisted scum'.

Like most rational people, I was not a fan of racist humour, but nor was I particularly offended by it or ultra-sensitive about it. I can appreciate that someone making a racist joke might be no more racist than someone making a joke about necrophilia passes their evenings entertaining corpses. Too many people seek offence when it is not intended, particularly by proxy. If you seek offence, you usually will find it.

My only issue was I found the presumption that I was receptive to such nonsense to be impertinent.

Ben considered himself well-travelled, and he was in so far as wandering around the world in army accommodation and shouting at subordinates who could not shout back was travel. He'd been lucky and served at pretty much the least volatile time in history, so had never actually seen action. He knew almost nothing of the world or other cultures, and any discussion with him would invariably lead to some banal army anecdote or another.

He once said to me that he had not achieved his rank in the services by being stupid. I replied that indeed he had not, and it was in fact much more likely to have been in spite of that characteristic that he had been relatively successful. It was a full forty minutes before he worked out what I meant and challenged me on what he eventually realised was a friendly jibe.

It didn't matter though. If people only spoke to others with congruous intelligence, wit, ability and social background there would be very few conversations. I tolerated Ben's down sides partly because I liked him and partly because we lived in a community full of very diverse and sometimes eccentric people.

I was always aware of my own failings, which Ben and others happily commented upon regularly but I did not see that as a reason to retaliate. Anyway, I did like the guy, not least because he was loyal and he was generous, qualities I admire in anyone, even the stupid and pretentious. When Ben was relaxed, and off guard, and forgetting his accent, not trying to impress he could actually be very good company.

The man had taken early retirement but had to wait a few years for the pension to kick in, so in the meantime he was pretty broke. He had a lovely home and no debts and he and his fiancé got by picking up a bit of work here and there. I gave him a day or two labouring on the development from time to time.

Ben did not suffer from silly pride when it came to putting a meal on the table, and that was another thing I liked about him. He was not too special to roll up his sleeves and get stuck in, he was however as useless at construction as it was possible to be; enthusiastic but useless.

As time went by he dropped much of the affectation around Lucy and me and was pretty normal. We occasionally had BBQs and dinner at each other's homes when he would play the guitar and everyone would get drunk and listen to music or the crickets and frogs on long, warm summer evenings. He was great fun to be around when he was relaxed.

Although I have lots of memories of France and in a way the time there was challenging, particularly during the renovations, it did serve to give us both time and space to 'live-into' my condition. To get used to it and, by the way, to get used to being unemployed I suppose.

Unlike with Saint Francis school, I tend to recall the best of the times there, not the worst. I remember the long evenings in our beautiful gardens, listening to the frogs and watching storms arrive from the direction of the Bay of Biscay. My vegetable plot with Mollie, our westie, always resting near me while I worked, no matter how warm… the chickens and the geese, the market every Saturday, and the peace and quiet. We both knew it was never going to be forever however and the five years we had planned already was past. It was time to go home.

Chapter Sixteen

Going Home
(2009)

After almost six years running our little business in France, we were both ready to return to the UK. Although still hypomanic for most of the time I had learned a lot about how to manage my illness. My medication was Lithium and Lucy and both worked for me. I knew life would never exactly be normal but normal was never what I had been when you think about it; not even as a child. A lot of managing what you are is knowing who you are. I don't mean to sound philosophical but it's a fact.

At least the slide of my mental health had been stopped and whilst I was unlikely to climb all the way back up, I could make it part of the way. We'd both climbed ladders before. Maybe moving to France had helped, maybe it was the forced retirement, maybe Eamon finally being independent, Megan growing into an extraordinary young woman, maybe a combination of it all, who knows? Things were great.

One big reason we'd decided to return to the UK in 2009 was for Megan. Life for a young teenager in rural France was great, but for a young adolescent, starting Lycée it was not.

As I have said; the move to France was never intended to be anything other than a temporary move anyway, we'd planned maybe 5 years and had done 6, it was time for parole.

As it happens the decision was very timely. No sooner than we had sold up, the property market in France, along with that in the UK collapsed. We got lucky on the exchange rate coming home too as it was as good as it ever got in favour of the Euro. In addition, we bought our new home in a depressed market in the UK, I'd love to claim shrewdness but it was pure luck.

The return coincided with other things and it led to 2010 being a very difficult year for us all. Perhaps because Eamon had flown the nest and Megan soon would, Lucy had time to reflect, or maybe it was for some other reason. The years of trauma had taken their toll on her. Always the strong and stoic one in the family the rest of us had not noticed her decline. By the time the signs were obvious it was too late, way too late.

I'd stayed in France to conclude the sale of the property while Lucy and Megan returned home and rented a place in Crickhowell in South Wales and searched for something suitable in the country. The completion in France took almost a year and very nearly didn't happen as buyers were suddenly faced with the slump. It was time we had not intended to spend apart and stress we had not anticipated. I was home only once a month or so and neither of us were used to such long separations.

Lucy had moved from a set of ancient stone-built properties with nine bedrooms, a couple of acres of gardens, a pool and the peace and quiet of the French countryside to a two-bedroom rental in a small town in South Wales. Although only temporary it can't have been an easy transition for her or for Megan.

Perhaps Lucy had time to contemplate things, perhaps it all got too much, we shall never know but Megan came home from school one Friday to find her sitting on the end of her bed, her face four inches from the bedside lamp with the shade removed, staring at the bulb. She was untidy, unwashed and the house was a mess; it was so unlike her.

All the photos of the children had been removed and the washing machine was full of smashed crockery. She'd been writing pages and pages of gibberish, letters and numbers apparently meaningful to her and they were littered everywhere. Her breakdown was sudden and it was complete.

I was already on my way home due to the strange calls she had made to me, and within a few hours of me arriving she was in an ambulance. Her sisters and brother and brother-in-law apparently utterly clueless as to her obviously deteriorating condition.

She was sectioned under the Mental Health Act; it was a Saturday afternoon. It was one of the worst days of my life and probably not a great deal of fun for her. It really was absolutely terrifying. I knew a thing or two about mental health but had never seen such a sudden and extreme manifestation. The Lucy I knew was gone and I had no idea if she would ever be back.

Her psychosis was extreme and massively difficult to deal with initially. She was a different person, concerned with codes and numbers and curing the world of all its ills and of course, that ever-present virus of the mind; religion. If I could rid this planet of one thing it would be religion, if I got a second wish it would be to rid the world of those self-righteous deluded people who peddle it. On second thoughts that would be the other way around.

After the initial shock her condition was from time to time very funny. She was convinced that she was invisible but only when she had an elastic band around her wrist. Megan and I visited her in the hospital one morning to find her arguing with three other patients. All three were convinced they were the second coming and Lucy was at odds with them because she knew they were not, they could not be she claimed because her son, Eamon, most certainly was.

The weeks in hospital required Lucy to discuss her deepest troubles with therapists. She detested it and loathed pity yet no one could possibly hear her story and not feel that for her. The eventual diagnosis was not definitive but given the ordeal at the age of fourteen had never really been dealt with; it seemed a logical starting point.

Her childhood had been stopped in a moment and savagely ripped from her. Her potential and her future utterly destroyed. She'd come first in the county in her elven-plus exams aged 11 and was top of the class in Brecon Girl's Grammar aged 14 only to leave school a little over a year later with not a single certificate; it seems no one wondered why. No one asked what had happened, her mother's head too deeply buried in a bible to notice anything amiss. No one seemed to notice that she spent 9 years, from age 15 in an abusive and coercive relationship. Not one member of the family asked. I can't figure which is worse… the ignorant Welsh Baptists or the Catholic zealots my parents were.

The loss of Kirsty in such spectacularly tragic circumstances, the fifteen years of caring for her son and witnessing his struggles and pain, the failed IVF; then Eamon no longer needing her as he had over so many years, Megan soon to be leaving home also; all had taken their toll over the years. Then, finally with no worries, no problems of the conventional kind; her mind had let go.

Maybe because she knew no one needed to rely on her, and it was safe to finally collapse under the huge pressures she had for so long shouldered. Who knows? Her grip was not for her sake, it was for others, it was always, always for others. Every day I thought I could not love her more; every day I did, even in her worst state I loved her more, not because of it or in spite of it, just because of her. She even got ill with such spectacular grace and heroism.

It seemed to me that she might finally speak to someone qualified about it all but she still partly refused. She did however share more with me then about her past than she had previously.

Antipsychotic drugs, not free will. I knew of course what had happened and the dramatic effect it had on her life but had been spared the details, which were almost too hard to hear.

Ironically, but for that dreadful event, I would almost certainly never have met Lucy. I didn't pity her, I never pitied her, I wanted to and maybe should have, but she would not allow it and I respected and loved her more than enough to do as she wished in this thing…

But enough of the gloom.

Within a few months of Lucy being home, we bought an old house in the countryside in Monmouthshire and we immediately started renovating it. It had a small annex in which Eamon and Fiona lived for some eighteen months after qualifying as vets. It was great as it had land and was in the countryside and we'd got it at the right price. We even raised a few sheep there.

Access to Megan' school was simple and the annex proved perfect for Eamon and Fiona who in 2011 bought a Victorian Town house in Cardiff which I spent the next year renovating for them. They moved into Cardiff in 2012.

Eamon being back home, especially with his fiancé and Megan doing well at school was the best medicine Lucy could have.

Megan got into Swansea University in 2012 and graduated in 2016 with a BA in Modern Foreign Languages; she went on to do her Masters in Translation and Interpretation also at Swansea. By late 2019 she was living in Bristol working for a mental health charity, a job she loved but which paid poorly. She was also volunteering for a homeless charity. How on earth did I manage to have two such incredible children?

Lucy was again the absolute exemplification of contentment. Her both children were doing well, even if occasionally tattooed and boasting more earrings and studs than we would have liked.

Eamon married Fiona in 2014 and she had in turn produced little Edward on Christmas Day 2015. There was not even a hint from Lucy regards the significance of the date and his relationship to the almighty, which was a great relief to us all.

Chapter Seventeen

After
(2020)

Early in 2012 my uncle died and I bought his house from the estate with a view to renovating it and selling it to make some money. The house had been my maternal grandmother's and grandfather's and they had owned it since the 1930s when it was built.

I remember as a very small child climbing under the hedge from our own house, into their garden. In fact, it is my earliest memory. It's located about 100 yards from the sandpit on the top of Sarn Hill where I played when I was four or five.

I was born and lived for my first five years on the council estate which backed onto my gran's house. My mother grew up in the three-bedroom house in Heol Ganol along with her 15 siblings. When my brothers and I managed to infiltrate the 'private' sector we were rewarded by our gran with homemade fruit cake, so we named her house the 'Cake House'.

Also in 2012 Lucy, Megan and I moved to Maesteg, an ex-mining town in the Valleys of South Wales about twelve miles from the Cake House. We realised within a few months of moving that it had been a mistake. We had figured that a town house would be easier all round but almost immediately we missed the countryside. Together we spent most of our time in rural and semi-rural locations and before that I had spent a good portion of my childhood in the countryside or close to it. Town really was not for us; for one thing other people lived there, nearby, opposite, on both sides and behind, people everywhere.

When it came to buying the Cake House, the plan had been to complete it within a year, sell it and our own house and move back to the countryside. My brother Brandon, who lives in Ireland heard of the plan to renovate and asked to be involved so we purchased the place 50/50 with him.

The works on the Cake House were quite extensive and involved new floors, new windows, extensive remodelling new bathrooms, removing chimneys and so on. It took just over a year and I did all the work myself bar the plastering, which is a skill I simply have never been able to master. Brandon and I split the materials costs and when all was done, we sold it making a good profit which we split.

As work on the project was nearing completion Lucy and I made a big decision and bought a brand-new Jaguar XF. It wasn't the first new car we'd bought but it was the costliest and something of a frivolous purchase. Within just a few weeks of delivery of the car Lucy spotted a cottage for sale in one of the auction sites she used to scan regularly. It was in the countryside in Monmouthshire and secluded and was pretty much uninhabitable.

It's the way of these things I suppose that they tend to run a course which is sort of inevitable.

Within a few days we had driven up to the old cottage and with no one about we peeped through the letter box. It was actually two cottages made into one. It dated from around 1812 and was in a dreadful state. Located on about an acre of land it nestled half way down a little valley surrounded totally on all sides by nothing but countryside and woodland… and best of all - no people.

I've mentioned before how we always knew when a place was right. We knew better than ever that this was going to be our 'forever home'. What a nauseating phrase but so apt. I promise not to say 'dual aspect' or 'spacious and airy'.

The gardens were not just over grown, they were literally unnavigable. We could not cross them in any direction for shrubs that had grown into trees and trees that had variously over grown or fallen. Brambles the height of a man were almost everywhere. There were at least four forty-foot conifers perilously close to the building itself and several almost dead yew trees within feet of its foundations, presuming it had any.

The legal pack offered by the auction house might just as well have said; 'don't buy me'. The current owners, whose family had owned it since it was built, had asked the local planning authority if they could remove and replace the building and the council replied stating that the house absolutely could not be replaced. There was no water connection and the nearest mains were some 350m up a lane. There were numerous other problems, including a legal letter from a neighbouring farm complaining (quite rightly) about fence issues - It was perfect!

On the day of the auction just a week or so later we drove up to Cardiff and Lucy went in. I was not allowed because she worried I might get carried away and offer that which we could not afford, or maybe accidentally buy a pub or a bus depot or something. She by far is the most sensible one of us two.

Our absolute ceiling price was agreed and it was just 6K more than the guide price which incidentally we had already offered outside of auction to the vendor and they had turned it down.

Anyone who has been to a property auction knows that guide prices mean very little and the lots usually go for much more.

I drove around a little and arrived back just as Lucy was walking out of the hotel where the auction had taken place. I was aware that we had little to no chance. She asked me if I had proof of identification on me and when I asked why she told me that it was ours, for the guide price. Neither of us could believe it. We wondered why others could not see the potential.

The problem we then had was how to pay the full amount within 28 days. We had only a few weeks earlier bought the Jag and several months before that bought half a house with my brother. Even releasing investments, we were short by about £20k so ended up having to sell the new car at a considerable loss; the funds being released just in time. On October 13th 2013 we owned the cottage.

Though pretty much uninhabitable we spent the next several months travelling up every weekend to work on the land. We installed a wood burner and made it as cosy as possible and in a way, it was lovely and snug. The biggest difficulty was fresh water which we used to bring with us in 20L drums.

Bathwater from the well was brown and not something we wanted to drink. The odd weekend extended into the odd week and occasionally longer. It took a full eighteen months to clear the land. Eventually all that was left was the cottage and about seven years of wood for the wood burners. We then set about replanting hedges and the fruit trees and so on.

Planning had stated that no one could demolish and rebuild but even a cursory reading of the Local Development Plan suggested they were mistaken. I spent a couple of months putting together an appeal even before submitting the planning application as I anticipated refusal. I sent a copy to the council informally and then applied for permission. They granted us permission to demolish and rebuild with 50% more space.

I confess I was sort of relishing a scrap with the planners but they did not oblige. I am convinced that if that letter stating that permission would not be granted had not been in the legal pack we would never have got the place and certainly not at the price we did.

Lucy and I set about work as soon as we could. Both the house in Maesteg and the Cake House sold on the same day and we moved full time into the old cottage in March 2014. Megan came home the odd weekend and shared a tiny room with several spiders and mice.

First, while living in the cottage we built the garage and converted it into a sort of tiny flat. We bought a second-hand kitchen and used a few of the units, an old cooker and fridge and we took Lucy's mother's old bathroom out of her skip and fitted that.

With a little wood burner and a mattress, we could lay flat on the floor in the night and up against the wall behind a sofa in the day it was really very cosy. In fact, lying on the make shift bed in front of the wood burner watching late night TV was lovely and something I often remember fondly.

By this time the neighbouring farmer had not only allowed us access across his fields for a new mains water connection but had actually dug most of it and installed the pipe. He helped us numerous times during the build and proved to be an immeasurably useful neighbour without whose help the project would have been more challenging.

Next, we needed to remove the old cottages as the new house had to sit pretty much on the footprint of the old. Lucy and I removed the entire building, the roof, the walls, the timber stairs, windows, doors, everything. It took us exactly thirteen days from start to finish. We had help one day from her brother-in-law equipped with a sledge hammer, he was useless and spent the day criticising Lucy's mother, we decided not to ask him again.

Thanks again to the farmer and the use of his telehandler which he lent to us we were able to move a good deal of the stone walls into his field. Without that help the twelve lorry loads of rubble taken from site might well have been twenty, and a good deal more costly.

We managed to use all the bricks from the old cottage to build a solid accessway into one of the fields and reuse the old slate from the roof for covering the chicken house and two of the sheds. Doors, stone, timber and slabs were all repurposed, so we like to think that at least part of the old 1813 cottage is still here. We installed ground source energy system and later PV and battery storage. Maybe someone could make a program about such things one day.

We got the raft foundation into the ground by late October, just before the frost and we settled into our snug little garage for the winter of 2015. Could life get any better?

In April we build the concrete block shell. It was done in a matter of weeks, we employed a man to do the blockwork, Lucy insisted. I could have done it myself but frankly I am very slow with blockwork, and we wanted to get out of the garage.

Apart from the shell, the stonework and the plastering Lucy and I did everything ourselves. In went the wooden sash windows and up went the stonework. We manhandled the roof trusses onto the wall plates with the help of a neighbour. Lucy and I spaced and fixed them. I slated the roof, with Lucy climbing the scaffold and supplying me with slate - no small task.

We built the chimneys, did the leadwork, constructed oak fireplaces, laid the underfloor heating, built floors, bathrooms etc. and by September 2017 the whole thing was complete and signed off by Building Control.

Moving out of the garage was a relief, we had spent almost two years living in such close confines and working together every day. It is very fortunate that we like each other I suppose. Changing the garage back to a garage was bitter sweet and I think we both will always remember that time happily.

In the time we spent building the house we came to know several of our neighbours, some of whom are very nice and some are tolerable, given they are people. They have welcomed us here and it feels like home.

We live in a stone cottage in the countryside. It has oak beams and fireplaces. Roses really do grow up the wall and over the heritage green wooden sash window next to the front porch. We do not have bi-fold doors and our living room does not 'bring the outside in'.

I have a wife whom I adore and who seems fond of me. We have a son who by any reasonable reckoning should not be alive but yet is alive and thriving, and he has a wife and they have a son. We have a remarkable daughter who is totally unaware of how remarkable she is, but who is determined to drain us of our last penny, by one means or another. The latest being today, tickets for a festival she really MUST attend!

We have chickens in a run and a Romanian rescue dog named Layla and three cats named Bob, Kpo and Jess. We've built a Bread and Pizza oven in the garden and grow a few vegetables and raspberries and strawberries, figs, nectarines, grapes, apples pears, plums and the remnants of unsuccessful efforts to cook the pizzas are often seen flying over the hedge, accompanied by demonstrations of my extensive vocabulary of profanity. I bake bread and make jam and I am going to try to write a book, maybe a memoir and then a novel. I shall call it *The Execution, Life and Times of Patrick O'Donnell.*

Things are not perfect, but they are near as damn it. I have not forgotten from where I came, the journey I started alone and then shared with Lucy and I would not change a single thing of it, not a single thing, because it brought us to where we are.

I still remember the fear, and the unbearable and irreconcilable loss; that most of all. I remember myself as the boy who could not read but loved rice pudding and as the adolescent urchin who wondered off the tracks for a little while. All these things are still me and I will always be all these things. Most of all I am a husband and father, a good one I hope, it's all I have ever wanted to be.

I hope one day to develop a tolerance of other humans, but having met several, I confess I am not optimistic.